GUITAR ELECTRONICS
UNDERSTANDING WIRING

Timothy A. Swike

Please Read This FIRST

Terms of Use

Please send questions or comments to: indyebooks@aol.com

0-615 United States ISBN Agency

ISBN-13: 978-0-6151-6541-7

First Edition, September 2007

- 2 -

Contents

WIRING A STRAT

Let's talk about the legendary Stratocaster guitar. Personally, I don't think you can find a better sounding guitar anywhere. The unmistakeable strat sound is more tapered, with less highs and lows than other guitars, and it has more midrange. Much of the strat's popularity comes from it's hollow pickup cavity, and it's neck and middle pickups. It is perfect for playing the blues, jazz, or rock. These guitars are described by many as having a quacky, or even smokey sound. Now let's wire one.

TOOLS FOR THE JOB
First, we need to talk about the tools you will need for changing your electronics.

1 - Output jack
3 - 250K pots
1 - .050µF capacitor
1 - 5-way lever switch
1 - guitar wire 22AWG, white
1 - guitar wire 22AWG, black
1 - 25+ Watt soldering iron
1 - phillips screwdriver
1 - wire cutting and stripping tool
1 - rosin core solder

ASSEMBLING THE PICKGUARD
Install the potentiometers, or pots, and the 5-way switch in the pickguard. When the pickguard is upside down, the spring on the 5-way switch will be facing away from the pickups. Align the two tone pots so that the lugs are facing each other. The volume control will be closest to the pickups.

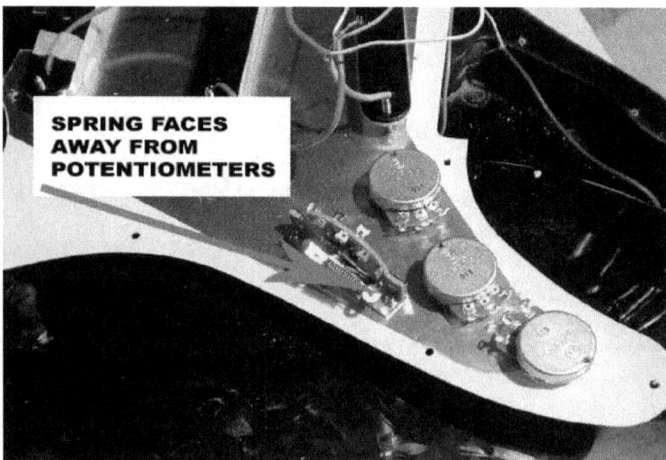

SPRING FACES AWAY FROM POTENTIOMETERS

HEATING UP THE SOLDERING IRON

Lets get the soldering iron ready. Plug it in and let it heat up in its holder. Remember, your soldering iron can get up to 700 degrees, or more, so be careful.

SOLDERING THE OUTPUT JACK

Next, we are going to solder the ground wire and hot wire to the output jack. The lug that connects to the prong is the hot connection. Solder the hot and ground wires to the output jack. Then screw the output jack into the guitar.

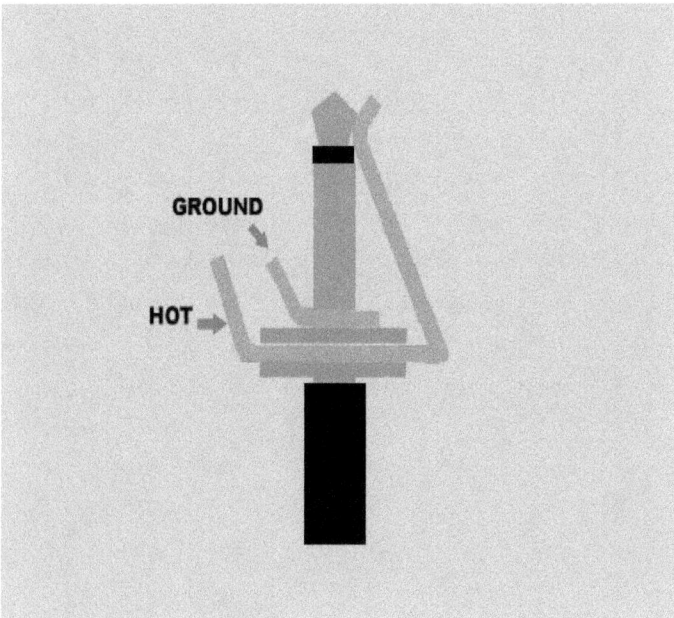

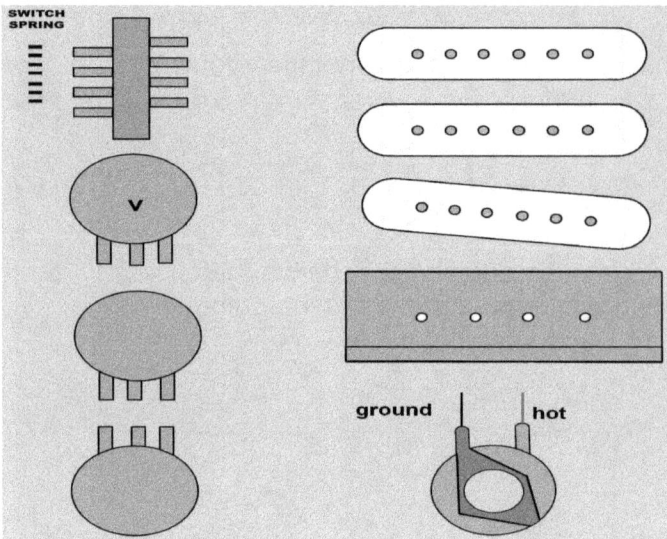

SOLDERING THE POTS

Add solder to the volume pot, and tone pot cases. All of the ground wires will be connected to each other on the pot cases. Now connect the far right volume pot lug to its own case. You can use a wire for this connection, or just bend the lug until it touches the case, and then add solder. Now add solder to the potentiometer cases. Solder the right volume pot lug to its case.

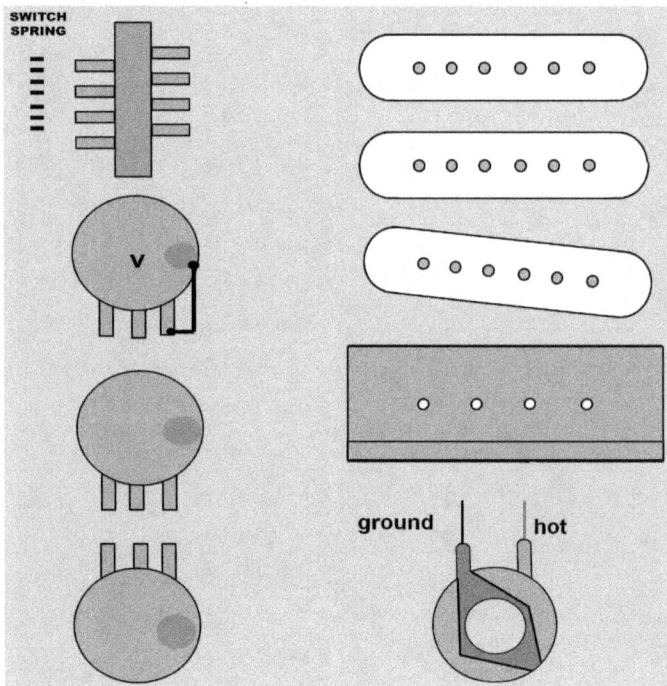

SOLDERING THE PICKUP GROUND WIRES

Find the 3 ground wires that come out of the pickups. Normally, they will be black wires, or they will be unshielded. The colored wires are usually the hot wires. Twist the three ground wires together and solder them to the volume pot case.

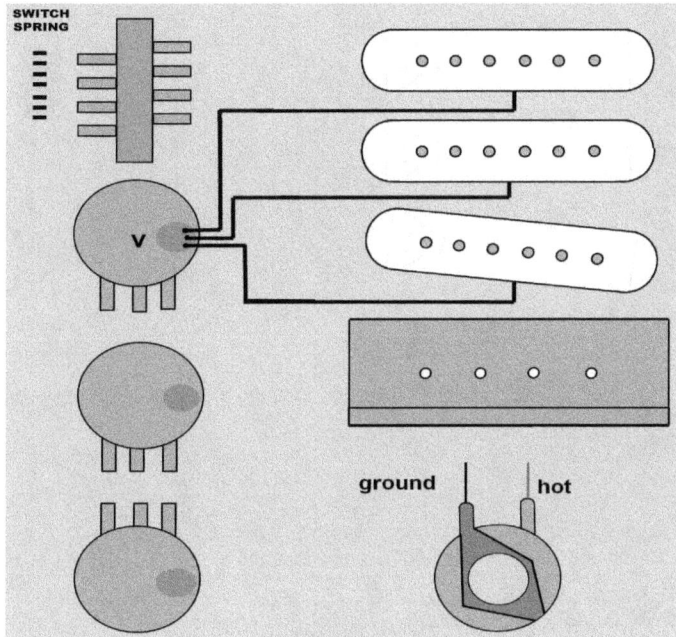

SOLDERING THE REST OF THE GROUND WIRES

Next, you are going to find the bridge ground wire and solder it to the volume pot. You are also going to solder the output jack wire to the volume pot. After that, you will connect the volume and tone pots with 2 more wires. The bridge ground will probably already be connected to the tremolo claw on the back of the guitar if you have a whammy bar. If it is not connected, you can always attach it to the bridge. All you have to do is send the wire under the bridge, and put it through one of the screw holes on the bridge. Then wrap the wire around one of the screws while it is being tightened down. This will prevent the bridge ground from moving.

Now connect the rest of the ground wires.

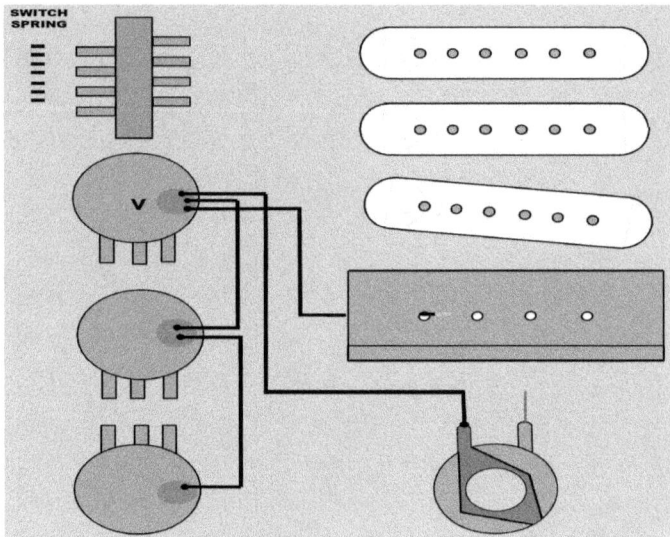

SOLDERING THE PICKUP HOT WIRES

Next, you will solder the hot wires from the pickups to the left side of the 5-way switch. Connect the neck pickup.

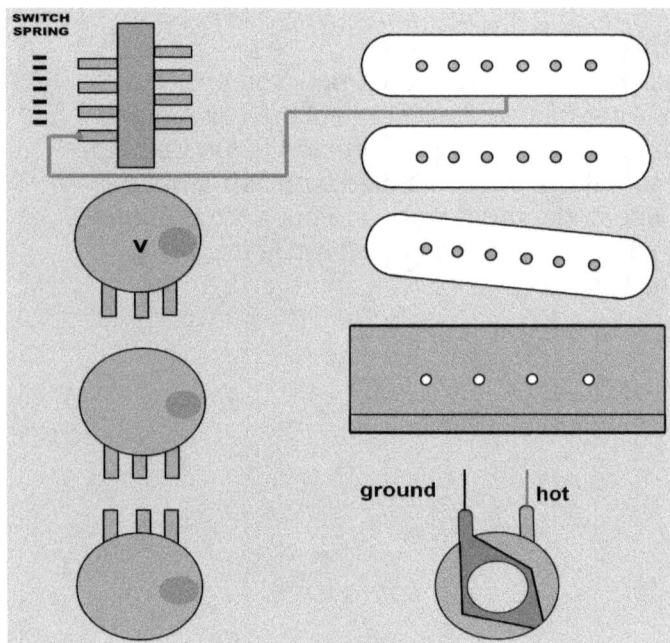

Next connect the middle pickup.

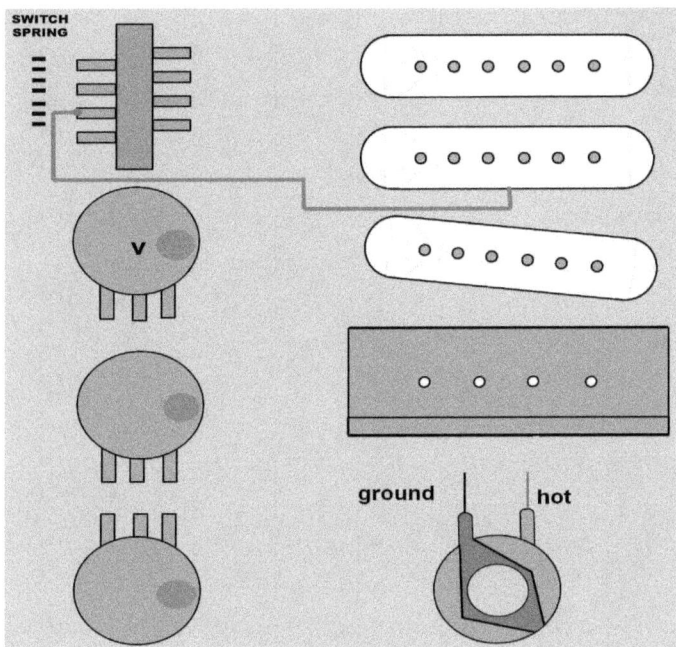

Now do the same to the bridge pickup.

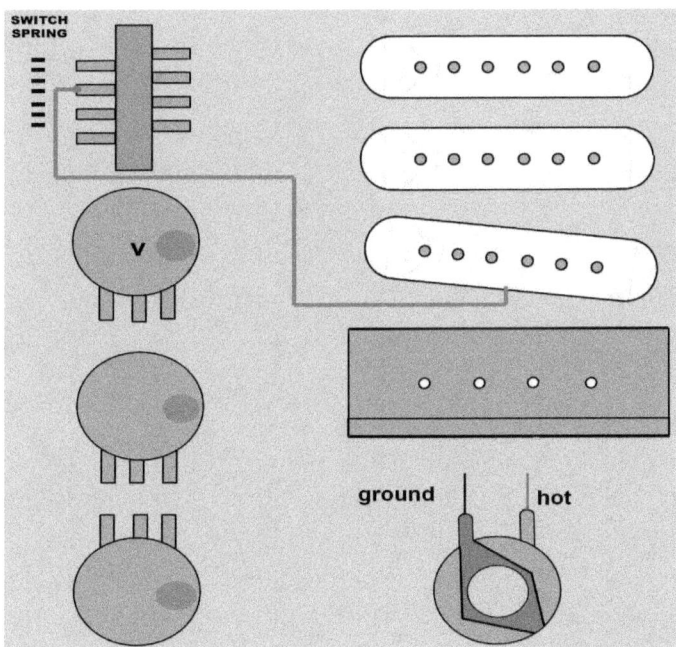

ADDING THE JUMPER

Now connect the top left lug to the bottom right lug on the 5-way switch. Twist another wire to the right lug wire, and solder it to the left volume pot lug. Also connect the left and right sides of the 5-way switch. Then connect them to the volume pot lug.

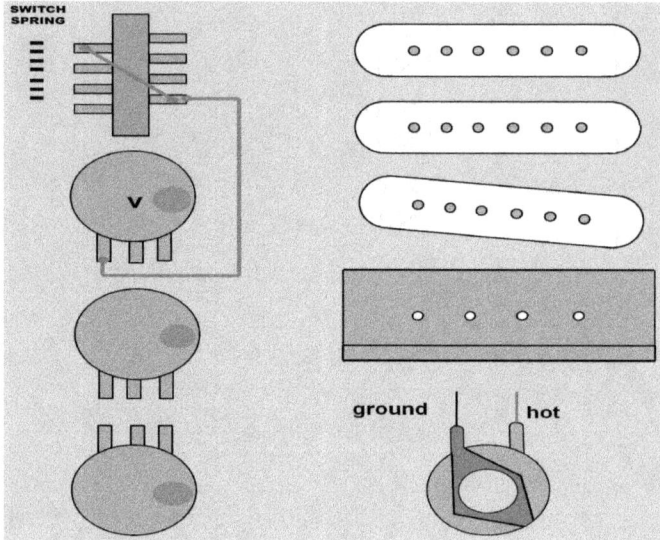

CONNECTING THE VOLUME POT TO THE OUTPUT

Now you can connect the middle volume pot lug to the output jack.

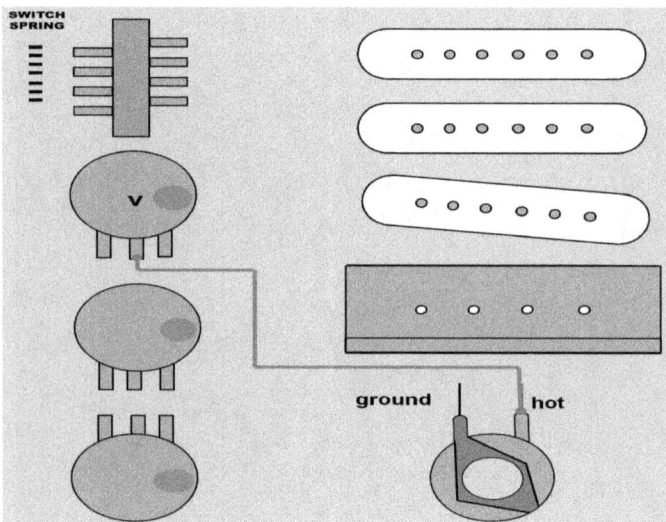

CONNECTING THE 5-WAY SWITCH TO THE TONE POTS

The next step involves soldering the switch to the middle tone pot lug.

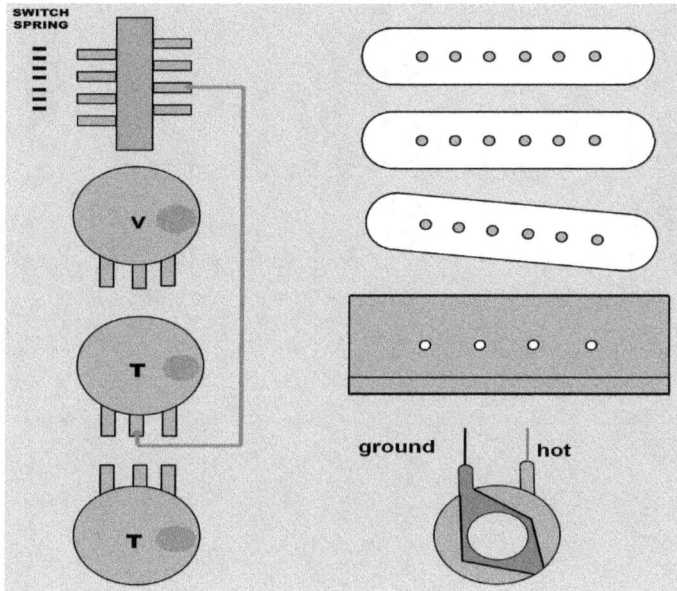

Next you are going to solder the 5-way switch to the bottom tone control. Connect it to the left lug. Also connect the switch to the bottom tone pot.

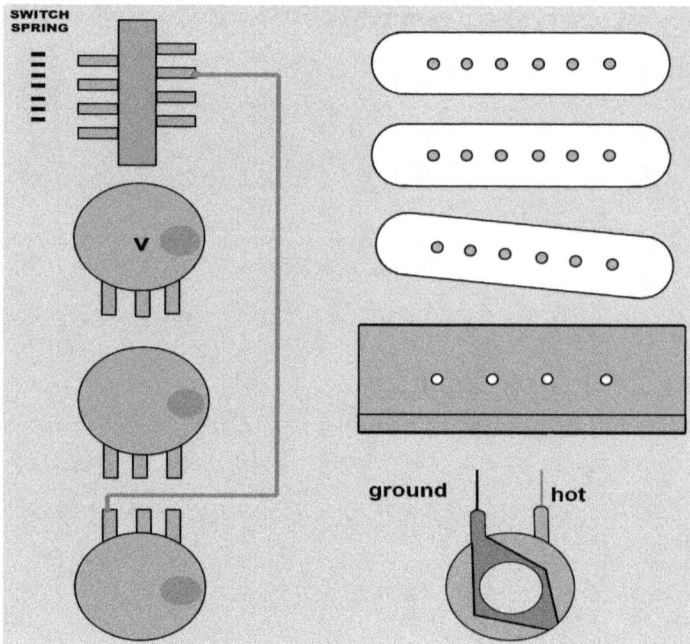

ADDING THE CAPACITOR

Solder the capacitor to the middle tone control. Remember, the stronger capacitor you use, the more bass your guitar will have. Connect the capacitor to the right lug on the middle tone control, then solder it to the case. That same lug will also connect to the middle lug on the bottom tone control.

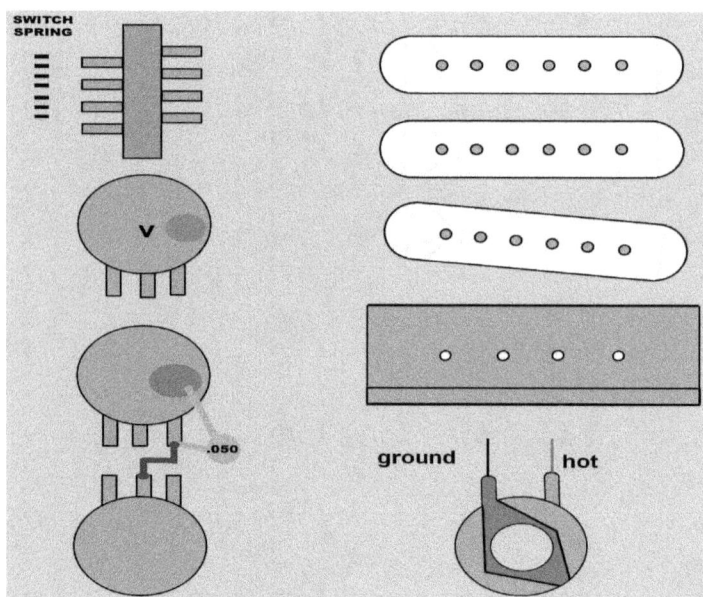

That's all there is to it. Here is the finished wiring.

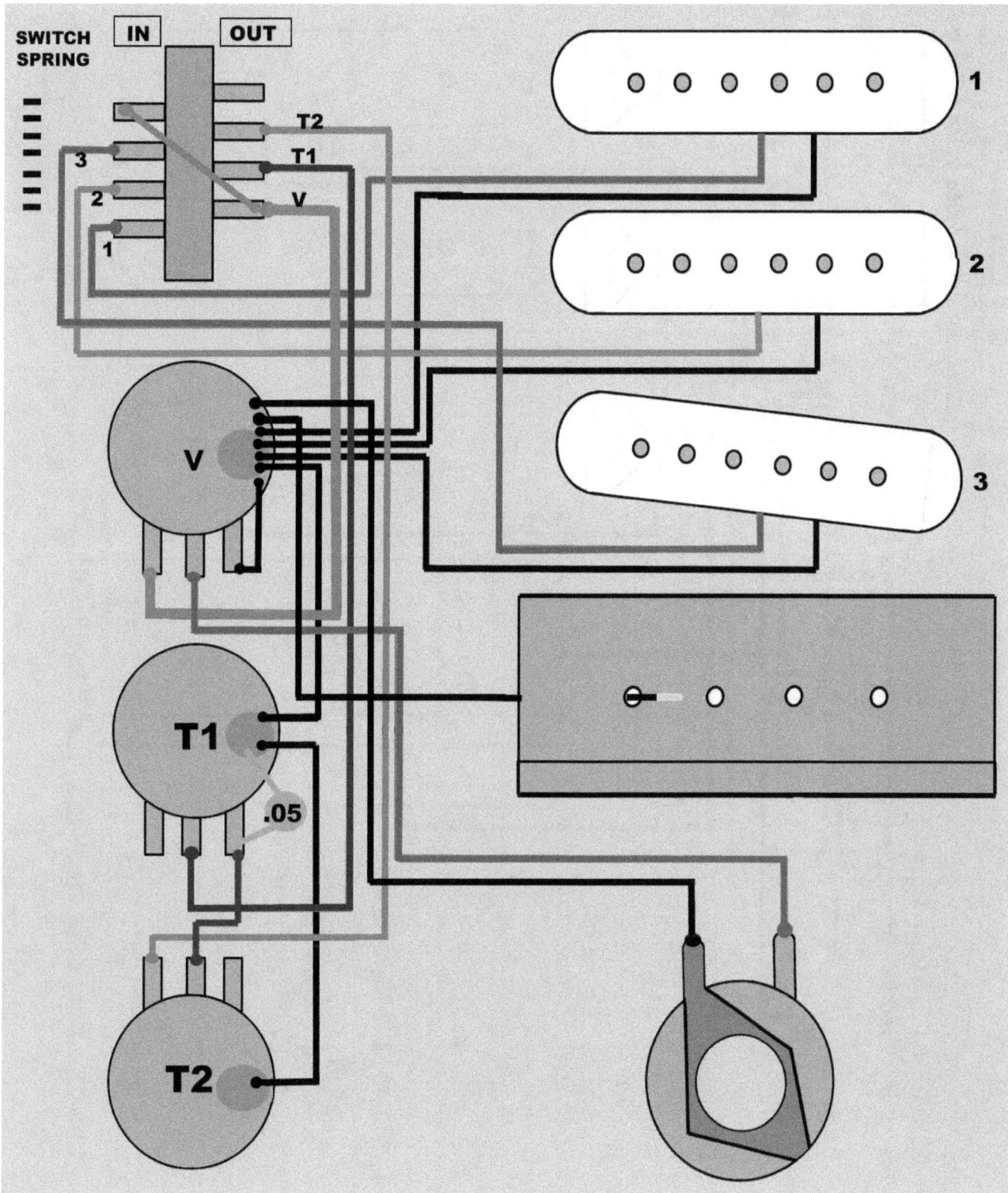

If you are using a megaswitch instead of a lever switch, then you can wire the guitar like this.

If you just wanted one master volume and tone control for all three pickups, you could wire the guitar like the diagram below. This would also give your bridge pickup a tone control. Notice a .01 capacitor has been added to the volume pot to take out some of the highs, and then put them back in the circuit before they go to the output. This prevents some of the highs from naturally bleeding out of a 250K pot.

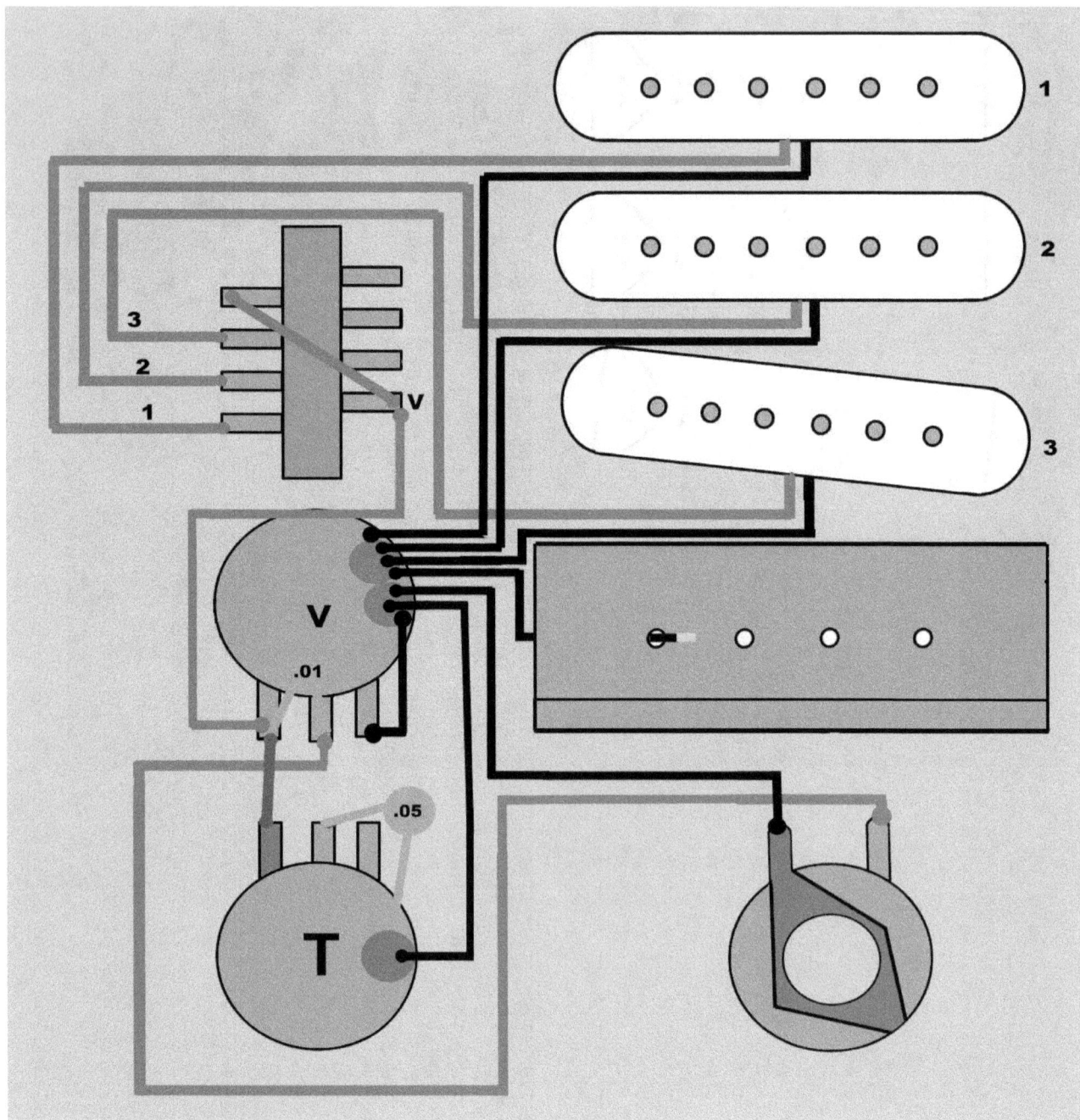

WIRING A TELE

The Telecaster guitar has a spiky sound, with more highs and lows than other guitars. It is well known for it's bright and twangy sound, that comes from the bridge pickup and solid body. It is loved by many for its ability to play country, bluegrass, and even the blues.

TOOLS FOR THE JOB
First, we need to talk about the tools you will need for changing your electronics.

1 - Output jack
2 - 250K pots
1 - .050µF capacitor
1 - .001µF capacitor
1 - 3-way lever switch
1 - guitar wire 22AWG, white
1 - guitar wire 22AWG, black
1 - 25+ Watt soldering iron
1 - phillips screwdriver
1 - wire cutting and stripping tool
1 - rosin core solder

ASSEMBLING THE CONTROL PLATE
The first step will be installing the potentiometers and 3-way switch in the control plate. When the control plate is upside down, the spring on the 3-way switch will be facing away from the guitar body. Align the two pots so that the lugs are facing each other.

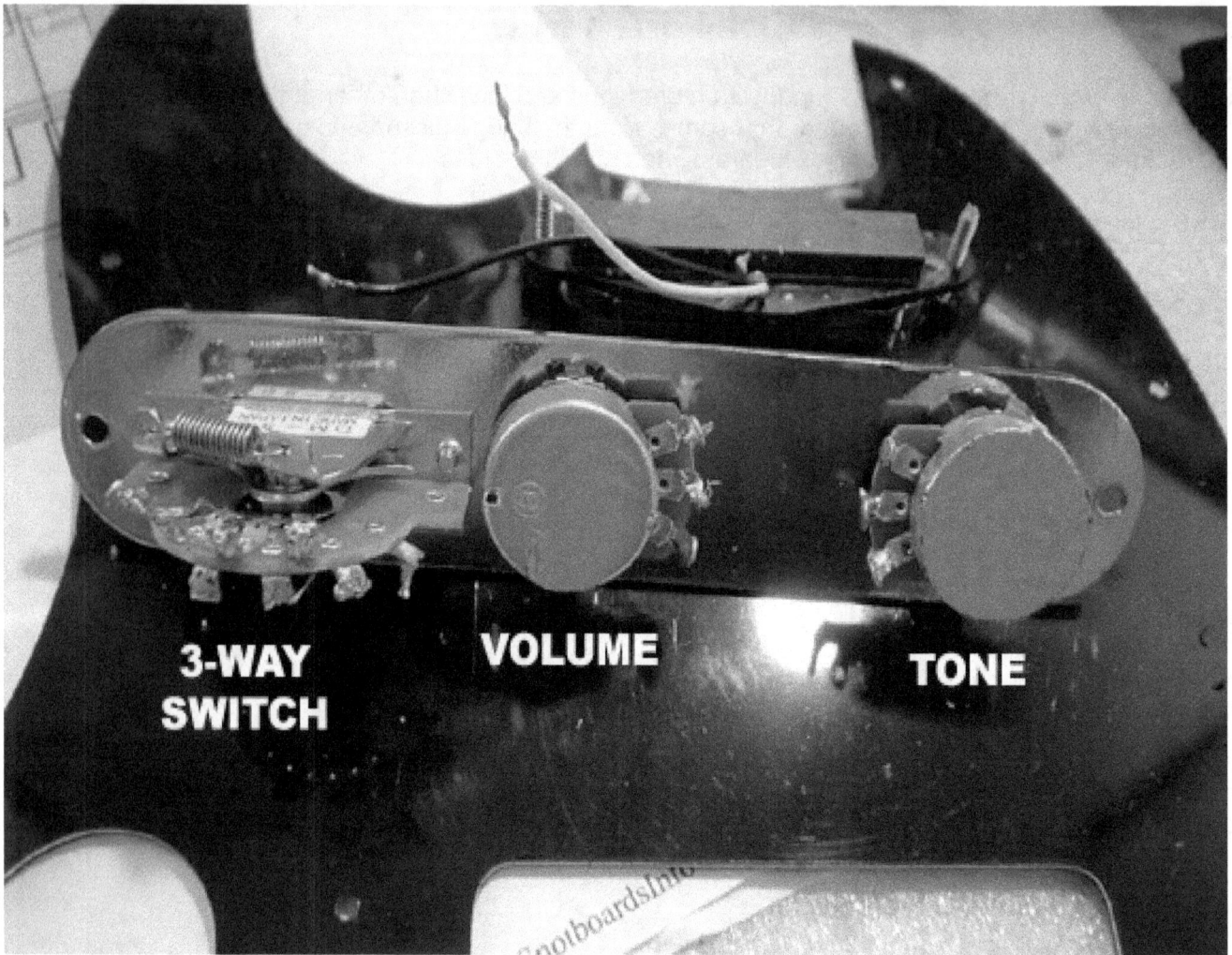

3-WAY SWITCH **VOLUME** **TONE**

SOLDERING THE OUTPUT JACK

Next, we are going to solder the ground wire and hot wire to the output jack. In order to solder properly, you should first add solder to each part that is getting connected. Then touch the two parts together along with the soldering iron. Make sure both parts don't move until they cool down, or else you will get a bad solder joint. It should only take a few seconds for the parts to cool down after they have been soldered.

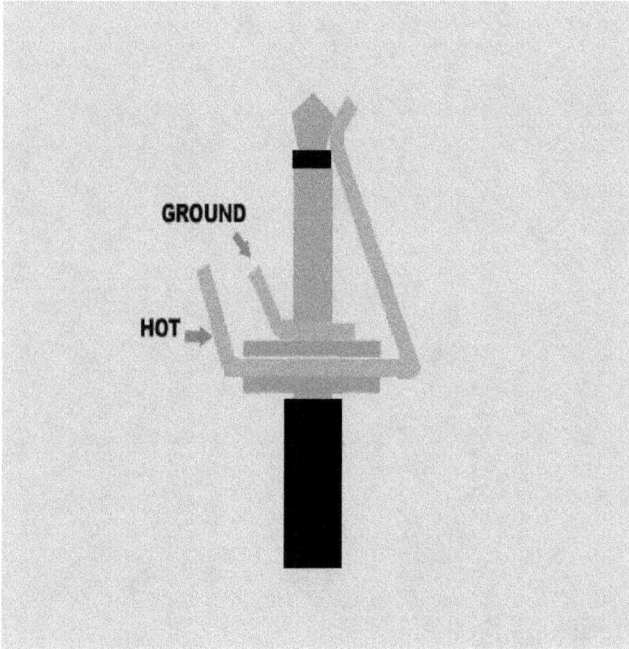

Next, fish all of the wires through the holes in the body. Pull in the output jack wires you just soldered, and screw in the output jack. Pull the bridge pickup wires through the hole closest to the bridge. Pull the neck pickup wires through the hole closest to the neck. Also add a black bridge ground wire that is going to go through the hole closest to the bridge. That wire will connect the bridge to the volume pot. Each pickup has a hot wire and a black ground wire. The output jack also has a hot wire and black ground wire.

SOLDERING THE PICKUP WIRES

The next step will be to connect the hot wires from the bridge pickup to the top two lugs on the right side of the 3-way switch. You can do this by twisting a small wire to the hot pickup wire. It is much easier to solder one connection to one lug. So if several wires need to be connected to the same lug or pot, twist them together before you solder them to the lug or case.

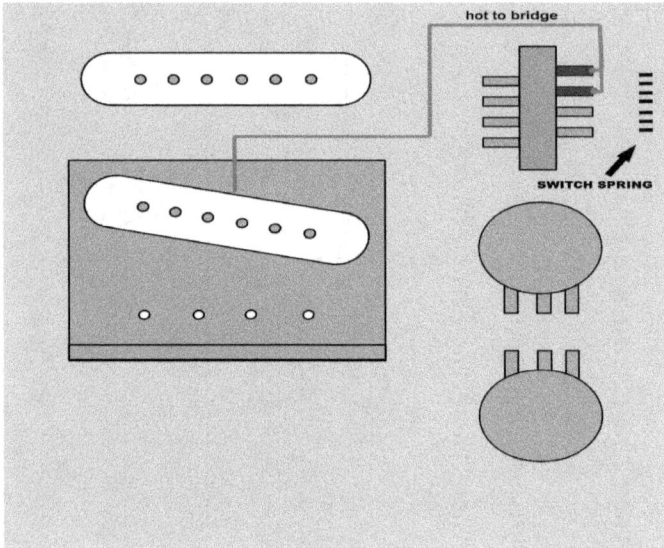

hot to bridge

SWITCH SPRING

Next, connect the hot wire from the neck pickup to the bottom lugs on the left side.

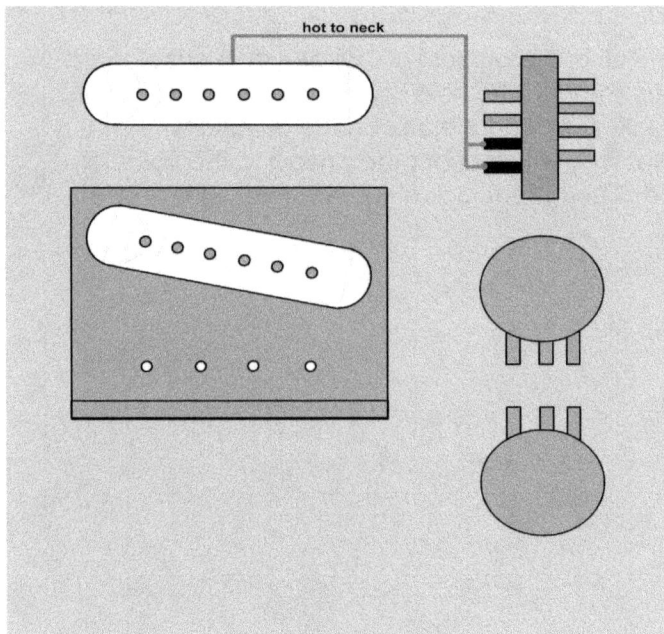

hot to neck

CONNECTING THE SWITCH TO THE VOLUME POT

Now you are going to connect the top left and bottom right lugs with a jumper wire. That wire will connect to the left lug on the volume pot, and also to the small capacitor. You will have to twist a few wires together to do this. Make sure to cut and strip the wires to the correct size.

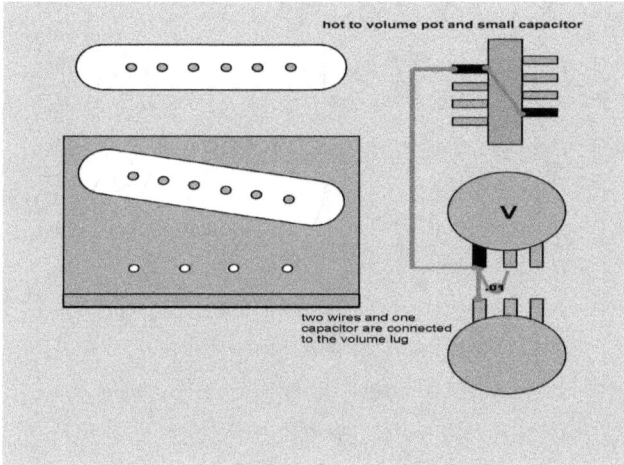

hot to volume pot and small capacitor

two wires and one capacitor are connected to the volume lug

SOLDERING THE VOLUME AND TONE POTS

The next step involves soldering the hot wire from the output jack to the middle lug on the volume pot. You will also be connecting the other end on the capacitor to that same lug.

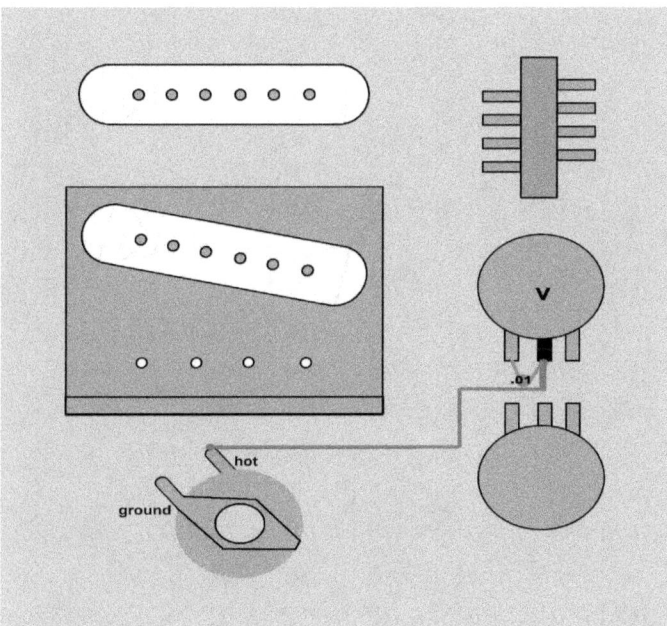

hot

ground

Now you will connect the loose bridge ground wire to the right side of the volume pot. Solder it to the metal casing. It will connect to another wire which goes to the right lug. That lug also will connect to one of the prongs on the large capacitor. Before you do this, you will need to add solder to the bottom of the volume pot case. Add solder to the left and right side.

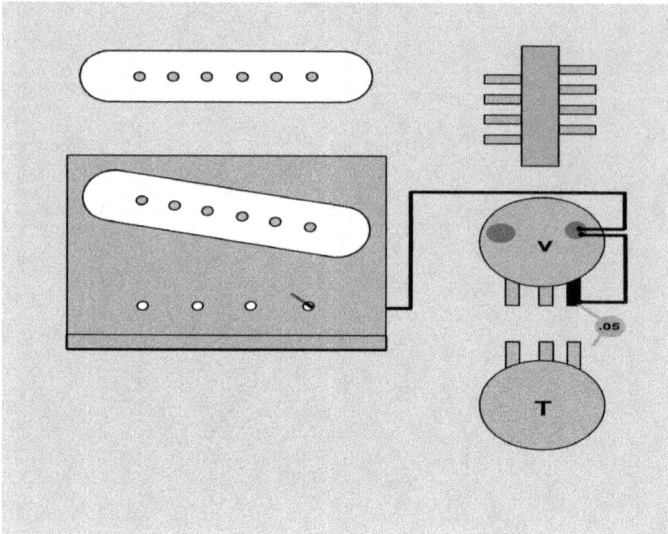

Next you are going to connect the left lug of the volume pot to the left lug of the tone pot. Also connect the right lug of the volume pot to the middle lug of the tone pot. You will also need to solder a ground wire connecting both pots as shown in the picture. All pots will need to be grounded, and all grounds will need to be connected.

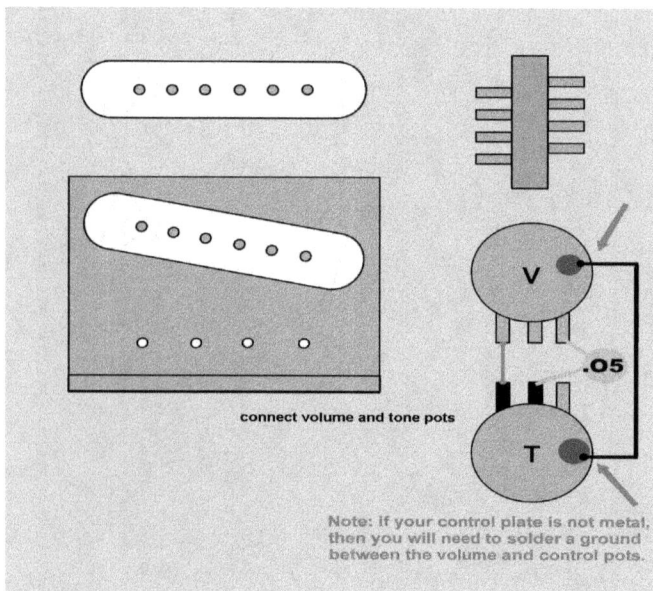

SOLDERING THE GROUND WIRES

Next, you are going to connect the three ground wires from the neck pickup, bridge pickup, and

- 22 -

output jack to the left side of the volume pot.

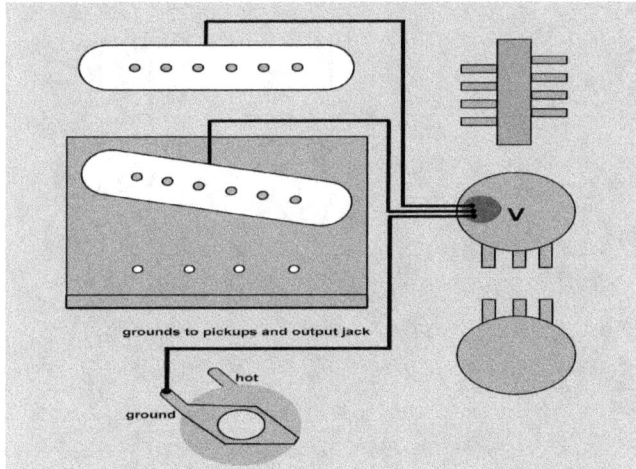

grounds to pickups and output jack

hot

ground

THE BRIDGE GROUND WIRE

The last step involves putting the black bridge ground wire through one of the screw holes in the bridge. Wrap it around one of the screws and screw it down. This way it will stay in contact with the bridge and won't move.

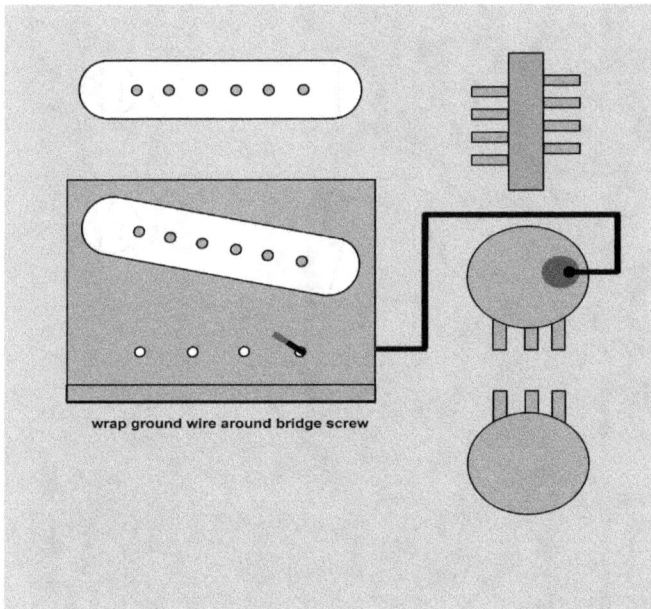

wrap ground wire around bridge screw

Here is the finished wiring.

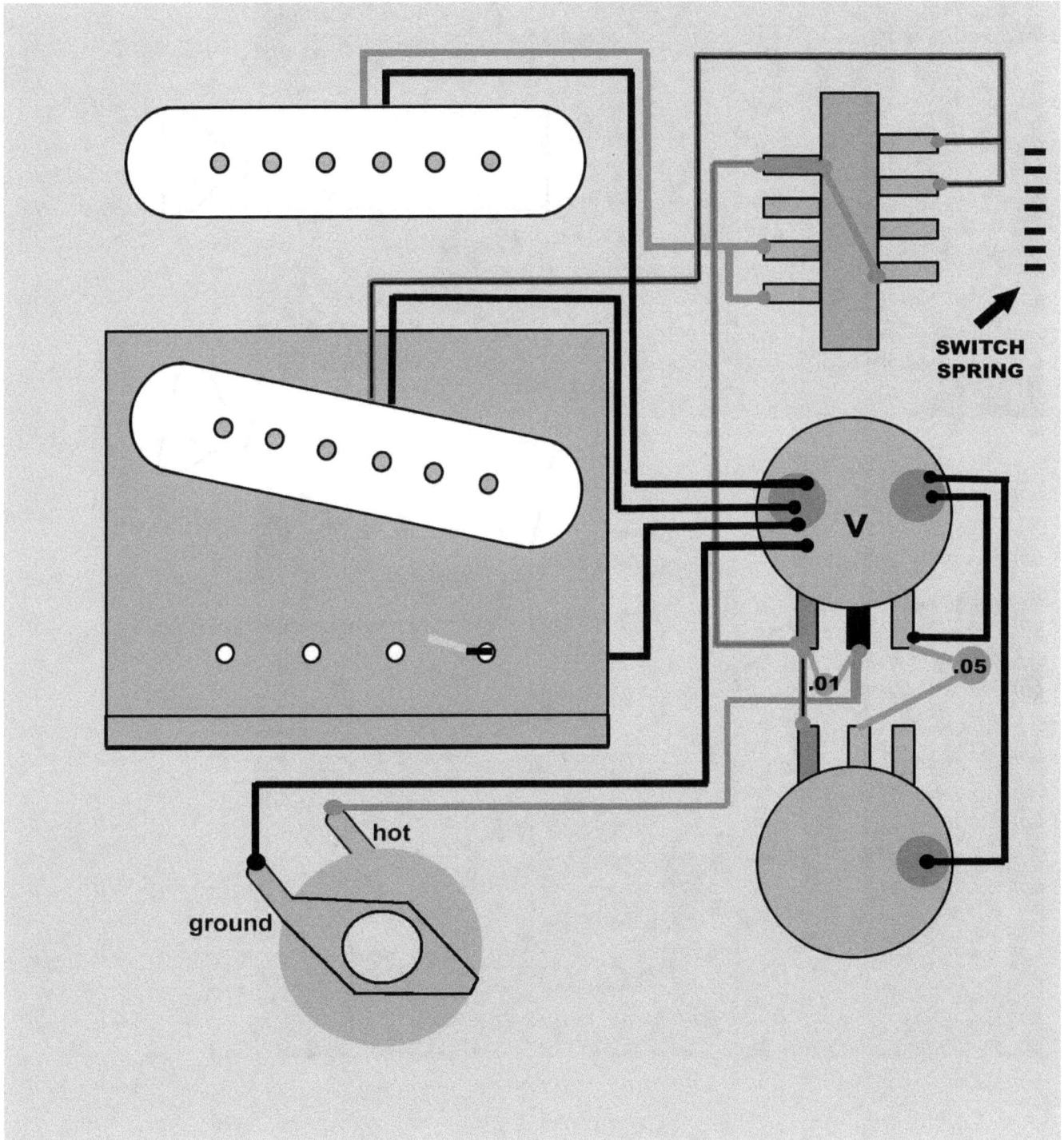

SWITCH
SPRING

V

.01

.05

hot

ground

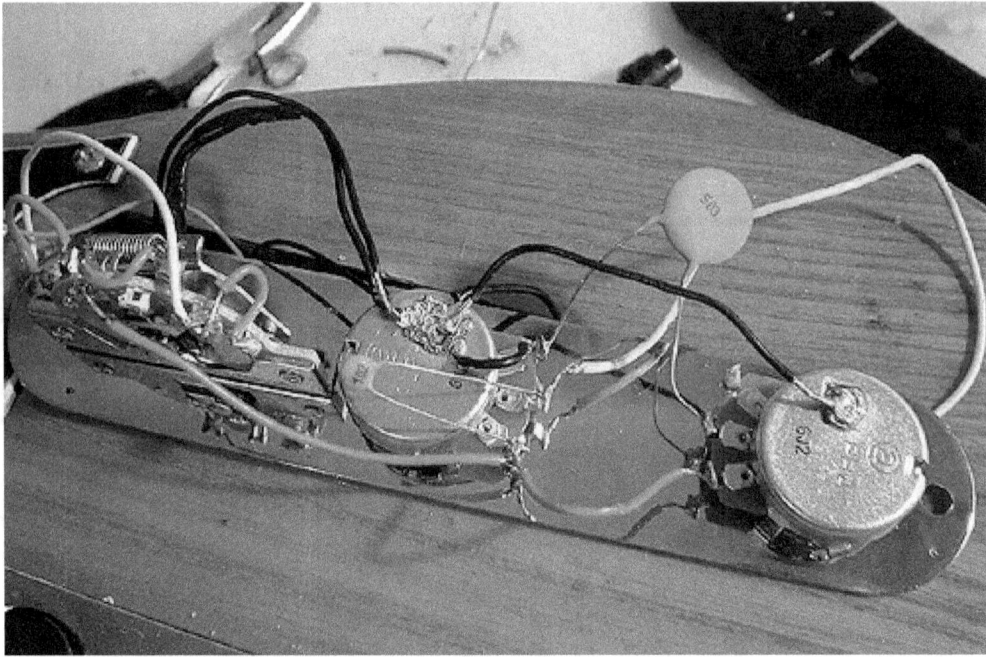

WIRING A LES PAUL

The Les Paul is THE guitar for playing rock music. Nothing will get your blood boiling more than one of these guitars combined with a vintage Marshall amp. The powerful les Paul humbucking pickups eliminate unwanted noise and give the guitar a fat and crisp sound. The mahogany body also helps shape the sound on this amazing guitar.

TOOLS FOR THE JOB
First, we need to talk about the tools you will need for changing your electronics.

1 - Output jack
4 - 500K pots
2 - .020µF capacitor
1 - Gibson toggle switch
1 - guitar wire 22AWG, white
1 - guitar wire 22AWG, black
1 - 25+ Watt soldering iron
1 - phillips screwdriver
1 - wire cutting and stripping tool
1 - rosin core solder

Now that you have an understanding of the strat and tele guitar wiring, let's look at the Les Paul. It's actually setup pretty similar to the telecaster wiring, with the addition of a toggle switch, and an extra volume and tone control. Also, the potentiometers are increased to 500K to bring out more of the highs. Take a look at how the rhythm pickup is wired. Each pickup follows this pattern. The pickup goes into the volume pot, then out to the tone control. The main output to the jack comes from the toggle switch. The tone pots have .020 uf capacitors which send the treble to ground.

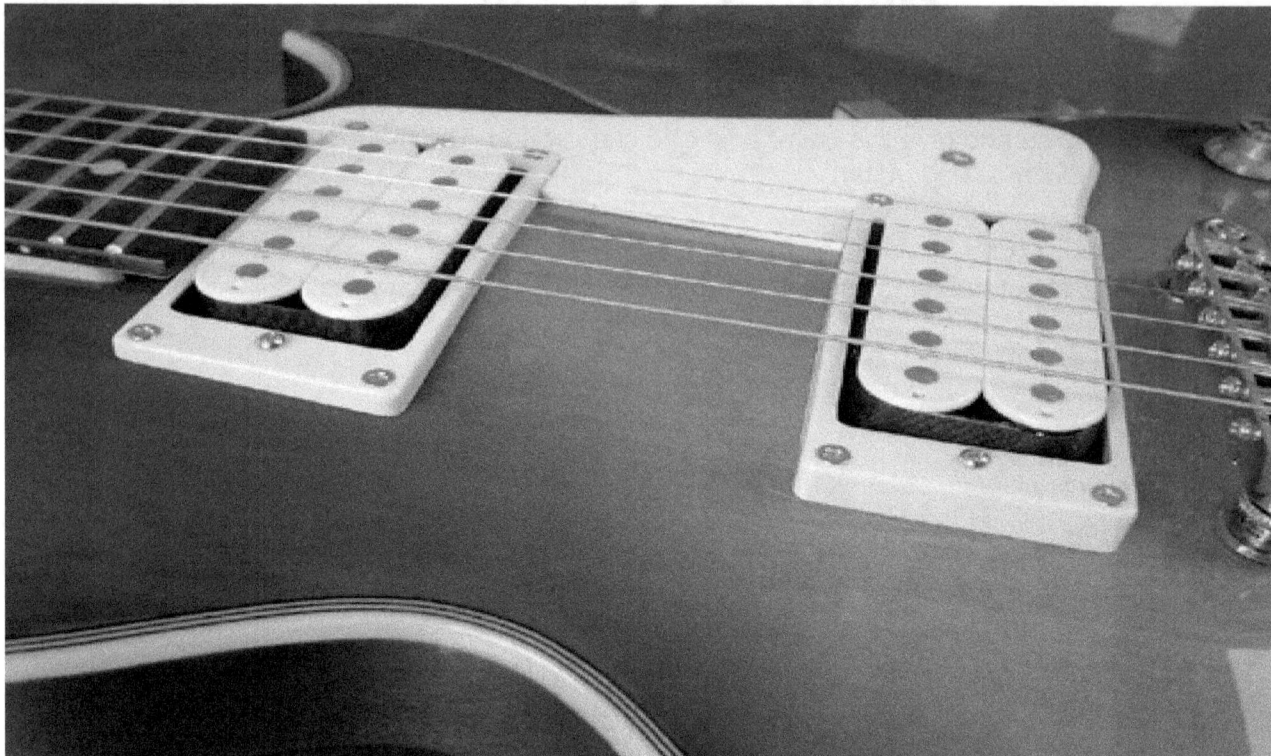

Notice how the toggle switch works. One side turns the treble pickup on, and the other side turns the rhythm pickup on. The two middle connections turn both pickups on. These inner two lugs need to be connected together. Some Gibson style toggle switches will have only three lugs, one for the treble pickup, one for the output, and one the rhythm pickup. The far left and far right toggle switch lugs will connect to the middle 2 volume pot lugs. Also, a ground wire will be attached to the back side of the toggle switch.

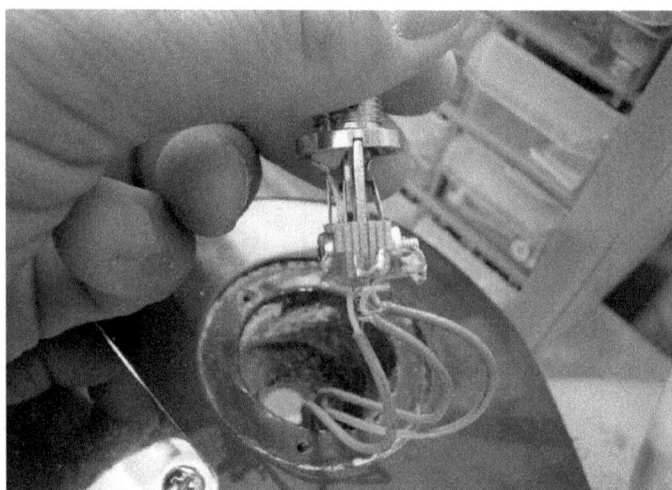

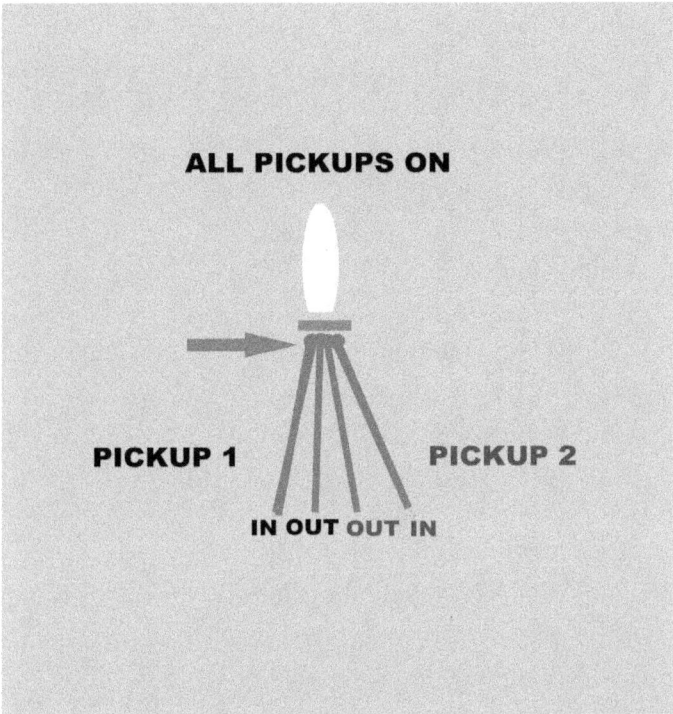

ALL PICKUPS ON

PICKUP 1   PICKUP 2

IN OUT OUT IN

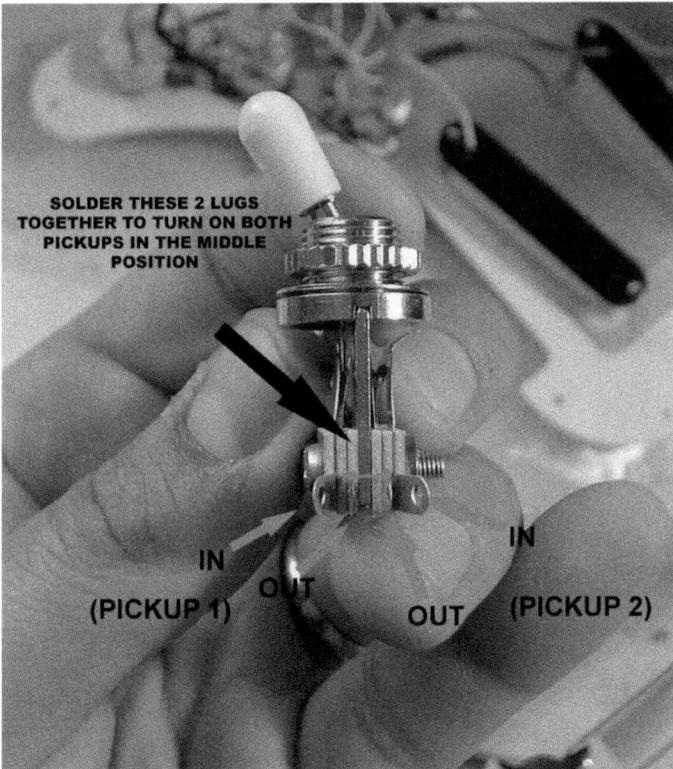

SOLDER THESE 2 LUGS
TOGETHER TO TURN ON BOTH
PICKUPS IN THE MIDDLE
POSITION

IN
(PICKUP 1)
OUT
OUT
IN
(PICKUP 2)

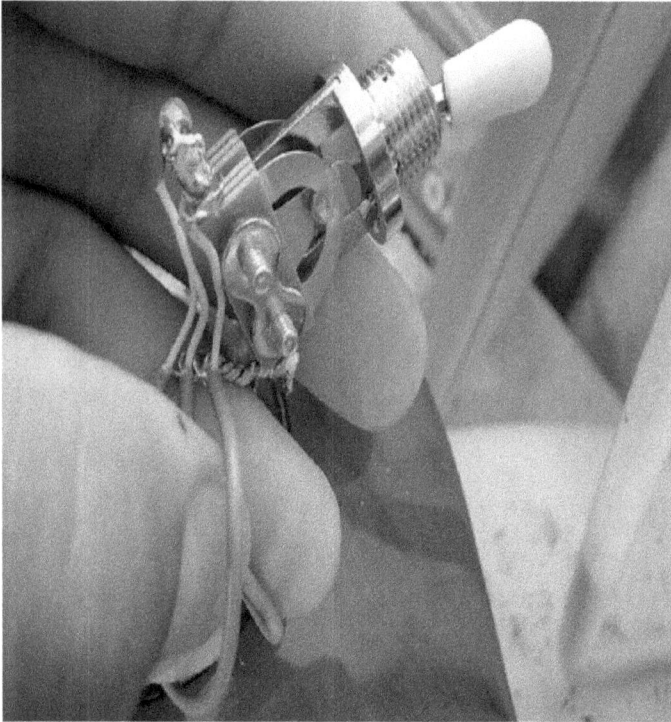

GROUND LUG

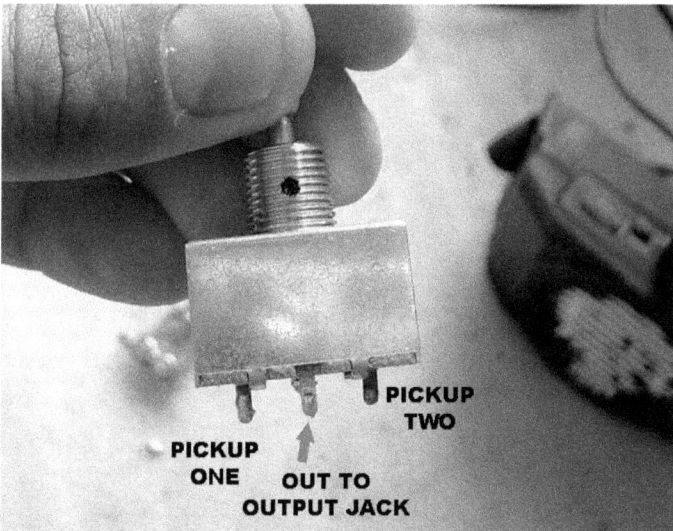

PICKUP
TWO

PICKUP
ONE   OUT TO
       OUTPUT JACK

The rest of the wiring is pretty simple. Add the .020 uf capacitors to the tone pots and make sure that every pot has a ground wire soldered to it's bottom. Also, solder the ground wire from the bridge post to one of the pots where the other ground wires are connected. The bridge ground wire needs to touch some part of the metal bridge, like one of the posts. All ground wires will need to be connected to each other. Don't forget to add a ground wire that connects to the ground lug on the output jack. And that's all there is to it.

Most of the wires in this photo are shielded in grey and black cables, so it is hard to see what's going on. The thick black cables house the pickup hot and ground wires.

Now take a look at the output jack. Both wires are shielded in a grey cable.

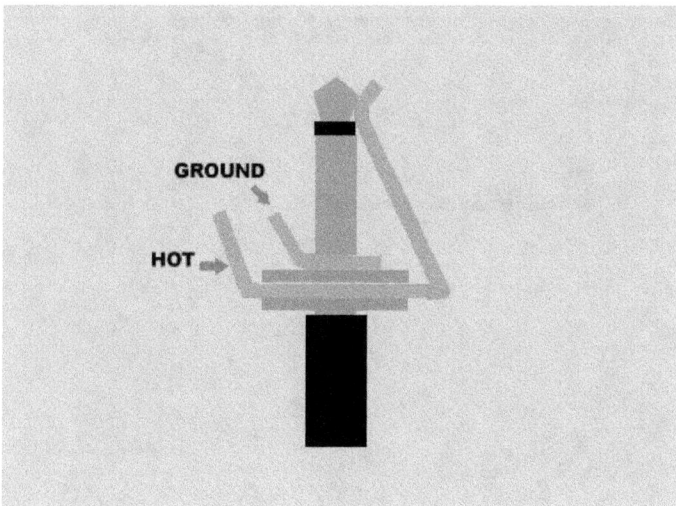

GROUND

HOT

Here is the finished wiring.

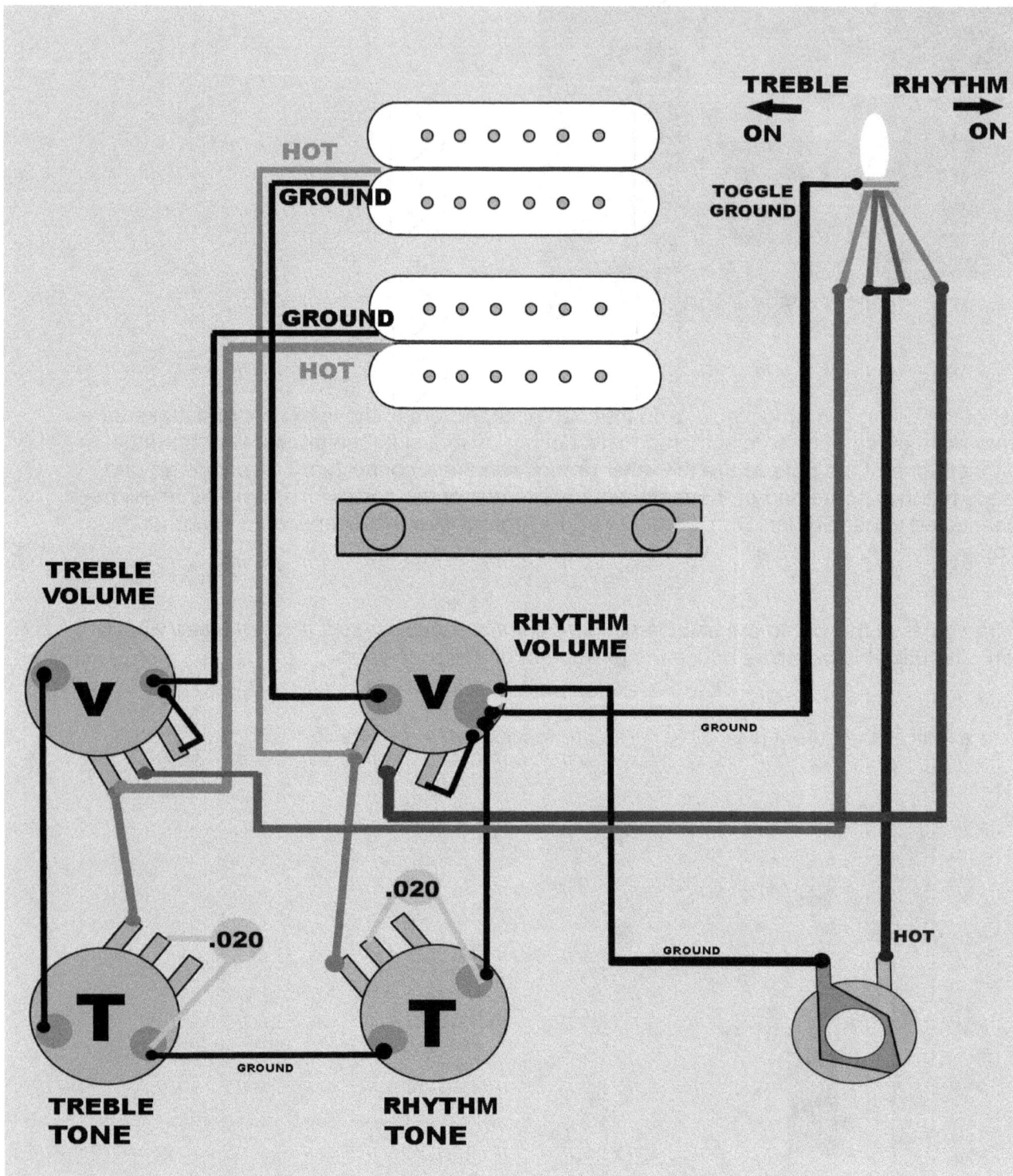

Note: if you have a 4 wire humbucking pickup, then you will need to connect the two finish wires together, unless you plan on hot rodding your guitar. Once the finish wires are connected, they will form a series link, which will be hum canceling. This will leave you with a hot wire that goes to the volume pot, and 2 ground wires that go to the volume pot case.

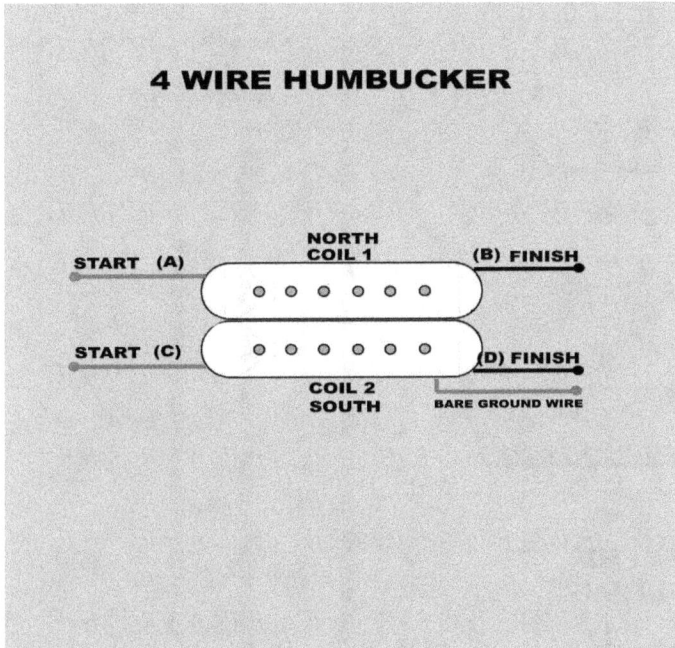

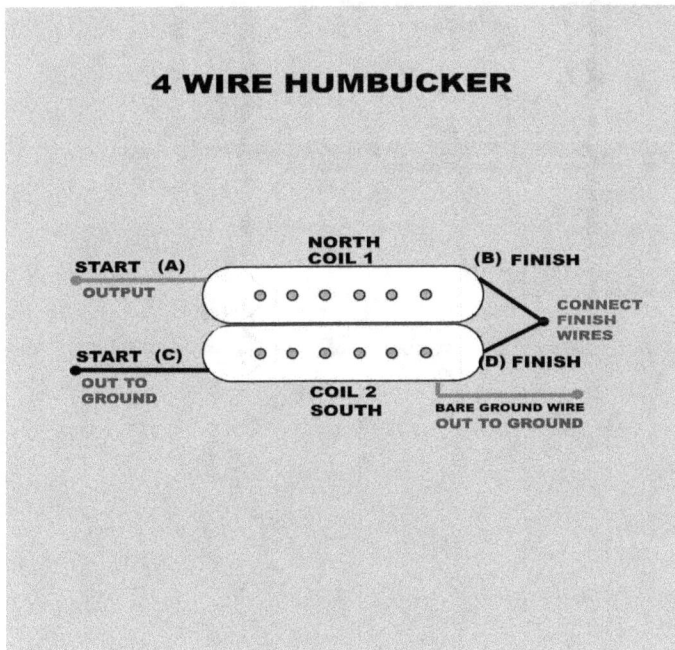

4 WIRE HUMBUCKER

NORTH
COIL 1

START (A)

(B) FINISH

START (C)

(D) FINISH

COIL 2
SOUTH

BARE GROUND WIRE

4 WIRE HUMBUCKER

NORTH
COIL 1

START (A)
OUTPUT

(B) FINISH

CONNECT
FINISH
WIRES

START (C)
OUT TO
GROUND

(D) FINISH

COIL 2
SOUTH

BARE GROUND WIRE
OUT TO GROUND

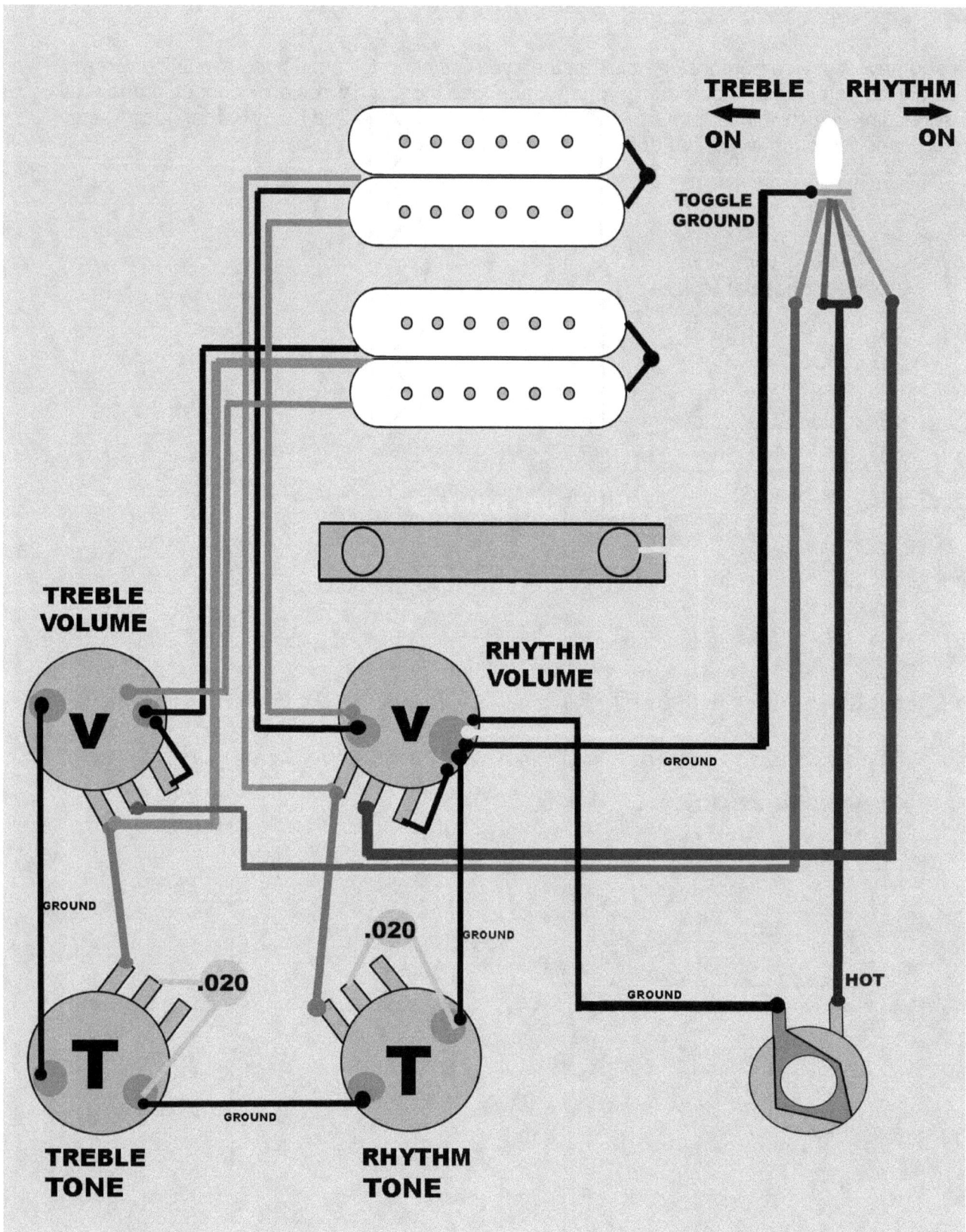

TREBLE
ON

RHYTHM
ON

TOGGLE
GROUND

TREBLE
VOLUME

RHYTHM
VOLUME

V

V

GROUND

GROUND

.020

.020

GROUND

GROUND

HOT

GROUND

T

T

TREBLE
TONE

RHYTHM
TONE

UNDERSTANDING SWITCHES

Almost every guitar has some type of switch on it. They are essential for turning things off and on. If you are going to be doing any type of wiring, then you are going to have to know your way around switches.

UNDERSTANDING 3-WAY SWITCHES

In order to wire 3-way switches, you first need to understand how they work. Basically, you have a hot wire from a pickup that goes into the switch, and a hot wire that goes out of the switch to the volume potentiometer. From there, the signal goes to the tone potentiometer and also out through the output jack. The 3-way switch will turn on or off each pickup. You have 3 combinations to choose from: the neck pickup on, both pickups on, or the bridge pickup on.

Now, notice where the neck pickup attaches to the 3-way switch. It attaches to two lugs. There are 8 lugs on the 3-way switch (4 per pole), so each pickup will need to hit 2 lugs, or else all of the pickups won't be activated when you hit the middle selection on the 3-way switch. The lugs colored in red show where the hot signal travels in each pickup selection. Any pickups connected to those red lugs will be on. Also, notice the jumper wire that connects the right and left side of the switch. This allows each pickup signal to exit out of the same lug, and connect to the volume potentiometer. Also, pay attention to where the switch spring is located when installing the 3 and 5-way switches.

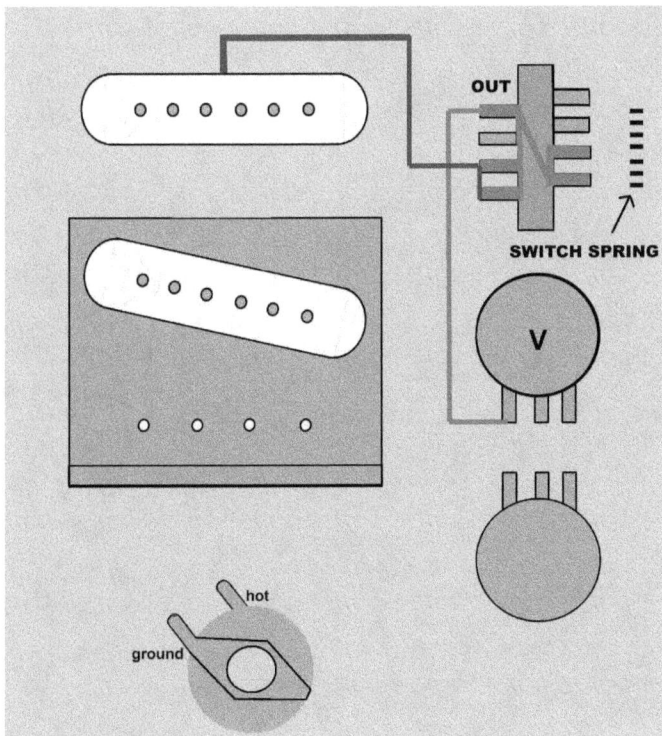

Here is a picture of the actual switch in the neck position. The red arrows show which lugs have the signal traveling through them.

NECK

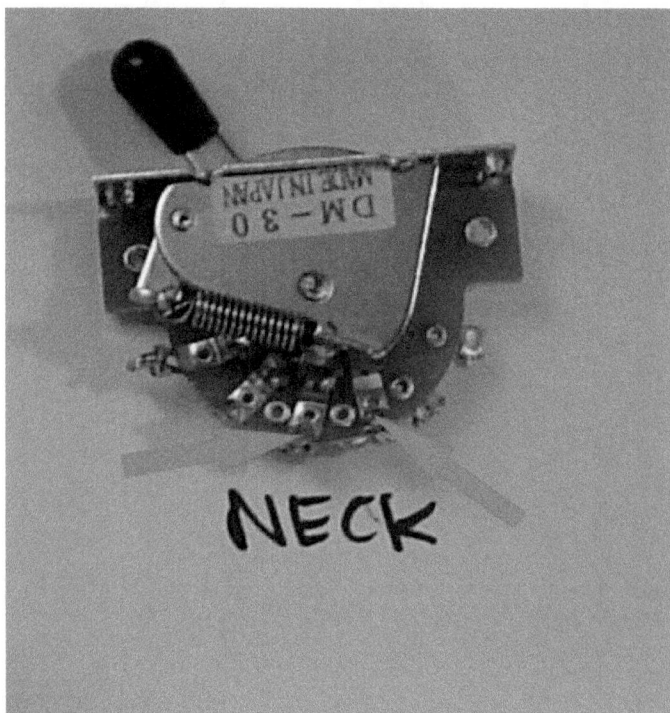

NECK

Now we are going to look at the switch when it is in the middle position. In this position, both pickups will be on. The bridge pickup connects to the opposite side of the switch.

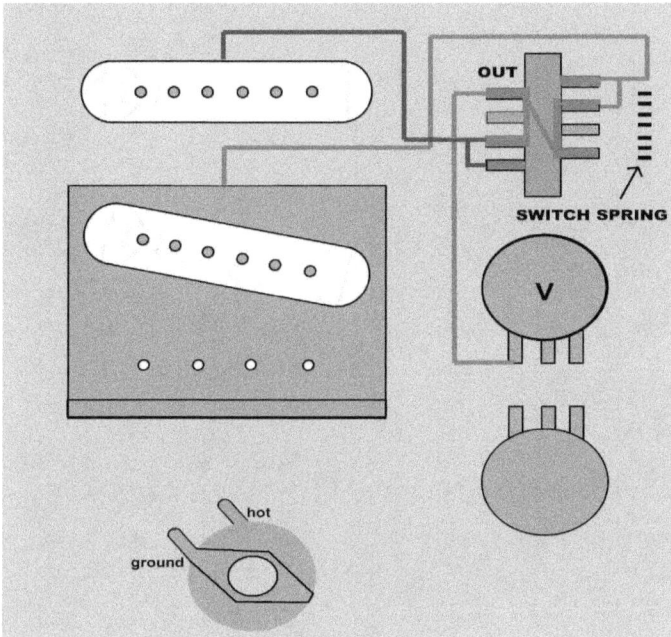

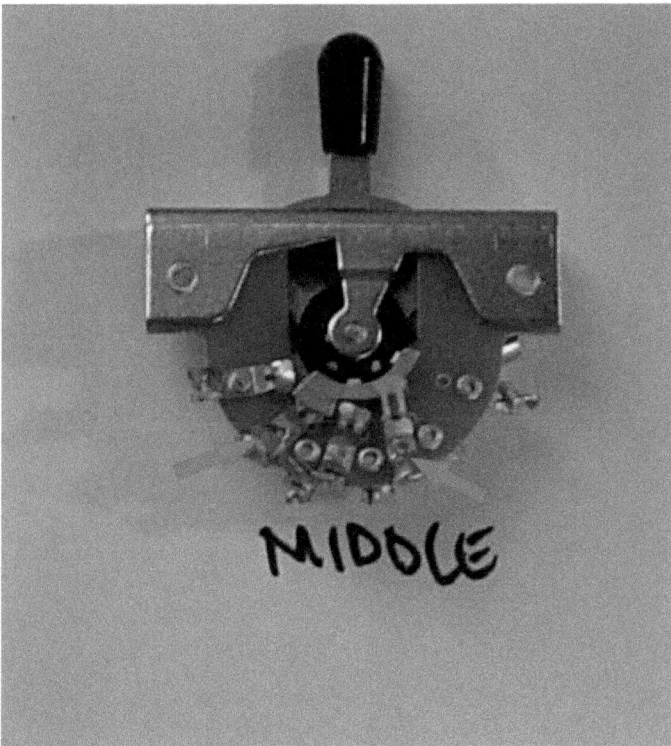

MIDDLE

MIDDLE

Now take a look at the bridge position.

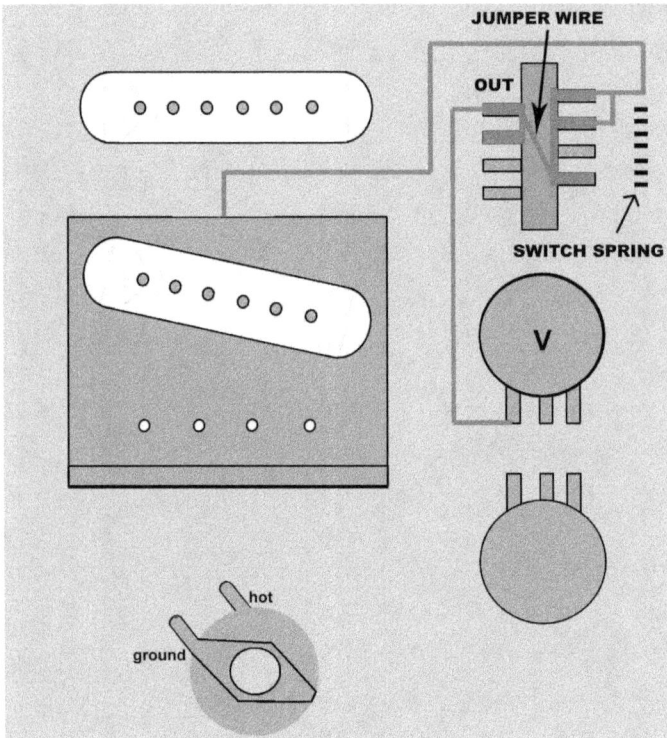

BRIDGE

BRIDGE

If you are looking for a 3-way switch designed to reduce unwanted noise, you can always try a **mega switch** by Schaler. Some guitarists prefer these to the standard spring action lever switches. I can't really notice much of a difference in these switches, besides the action in the lever. Wiring them is pretty simple.

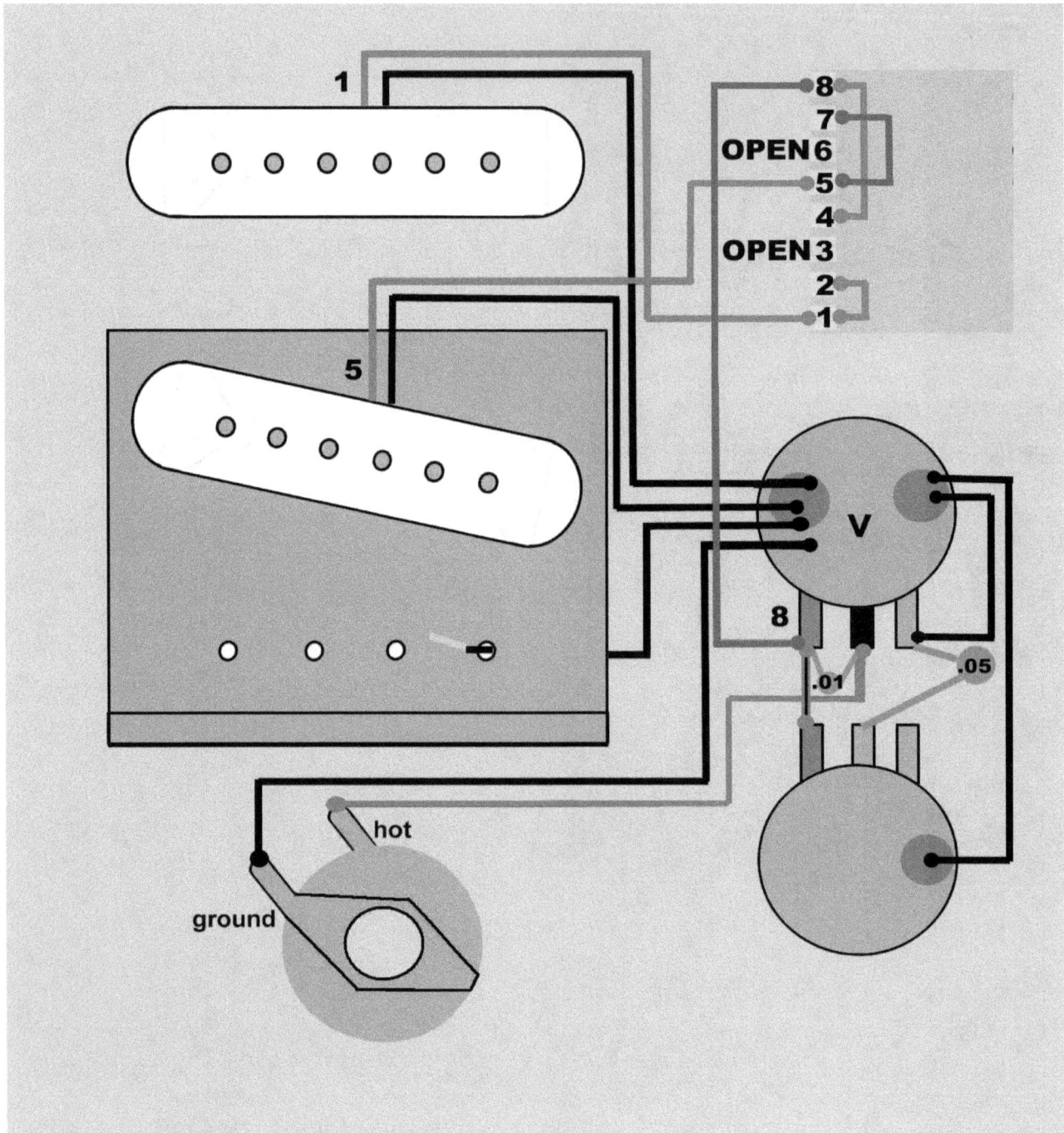

UNDERSTANDING 5-WAY SWITCHES

The 5-way switch is similar to the 3-way switch, with 4 lugs on each pole. It just has more lugs touching each other to come up with more combinations. Since there are 5 different pickup selections, each pickup connects to only one lug. The choices for this switch are: neck pickup, neck and middle pickups, middle pickup, middle and bridge pickups, and bridge pickup.

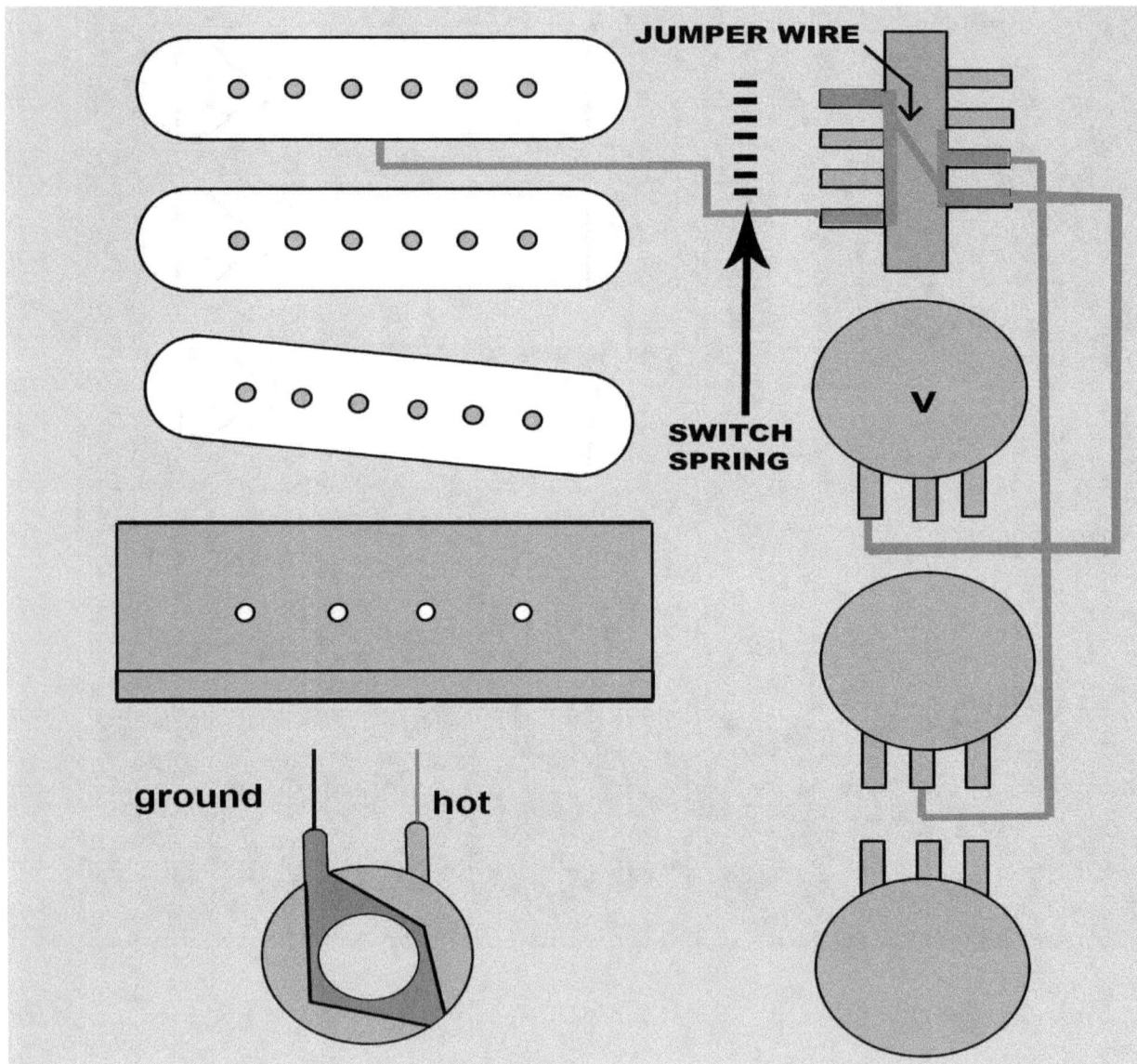

JUMPER WIRE

SWITCH SPRING

V

ground

hot

- 42 -

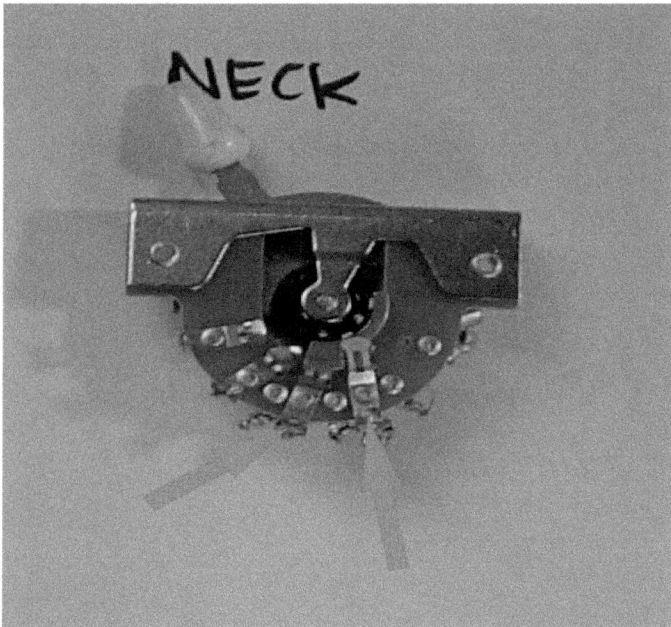

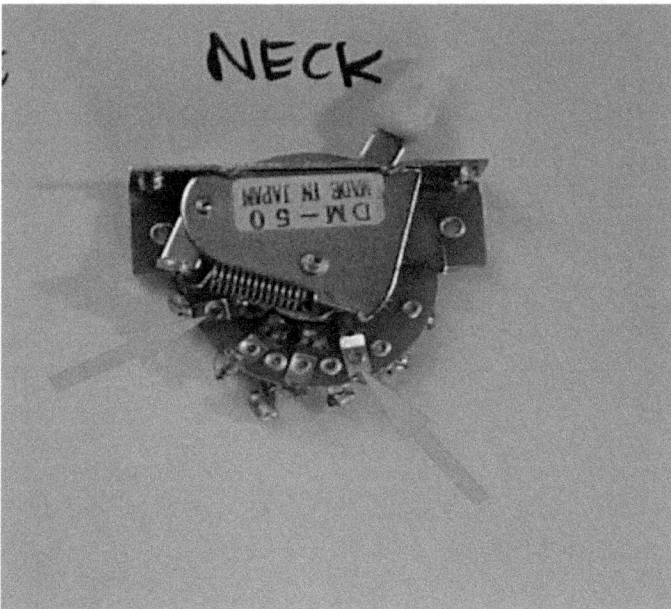

Notice the neck and middle position. Adding the middle pickup gives you more mid range.

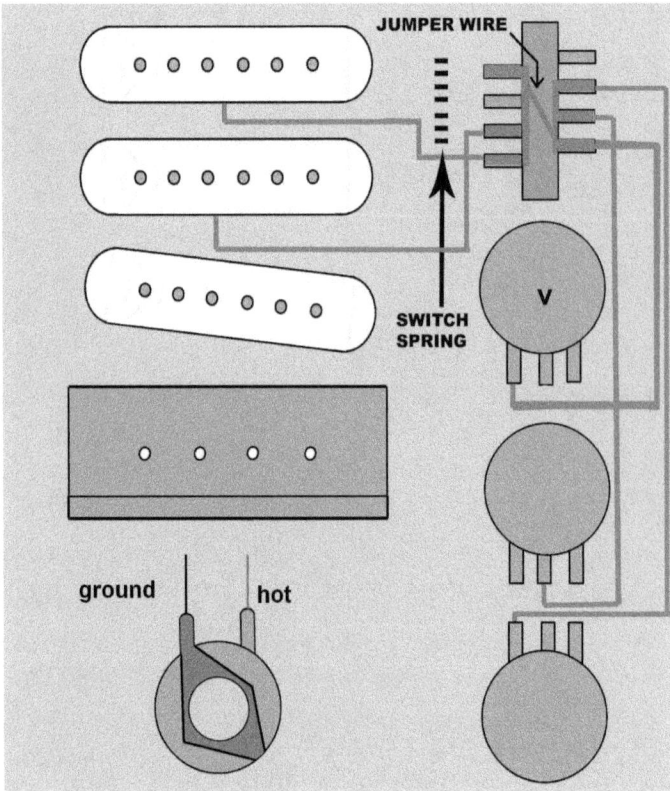

JUMPER WIRE

SWITCH
SPRING

ground   hot

V

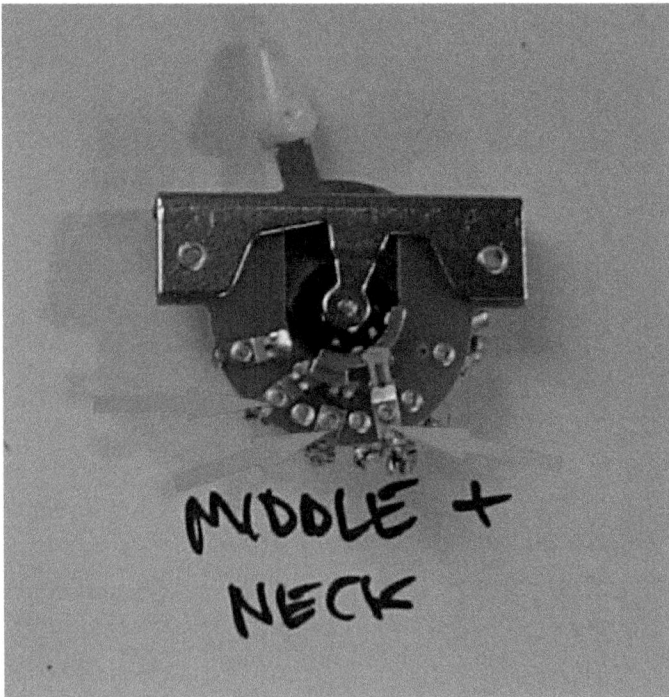

MIDDLE +
NECK

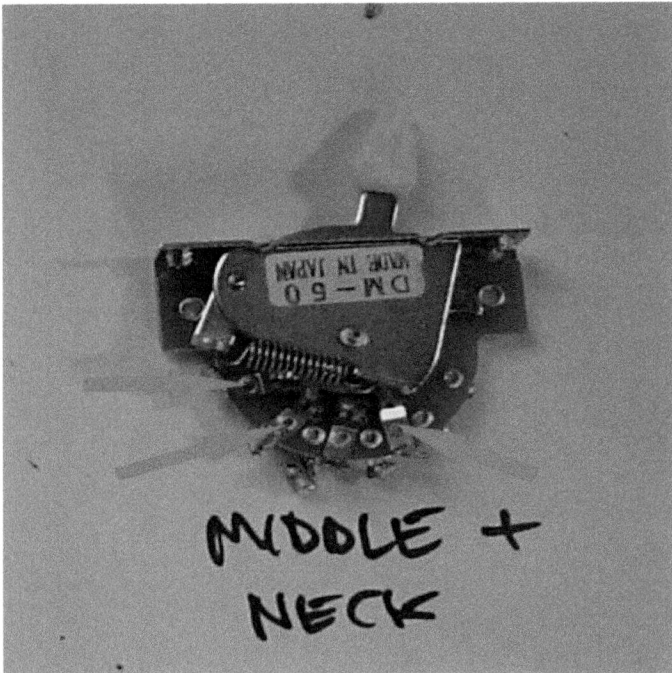

MIDDLE + NECK

Let's talk about the middle position. The hot signal enters the switch on one side and travels through the jumper cable and out to the volume and tone pot. The tone pot farthest away from the volume pot controls the middle pickup's tone. This pickup combination is probably the least exciting out of the 5 choices available. It lacks the highs and lows that the other combinations have.

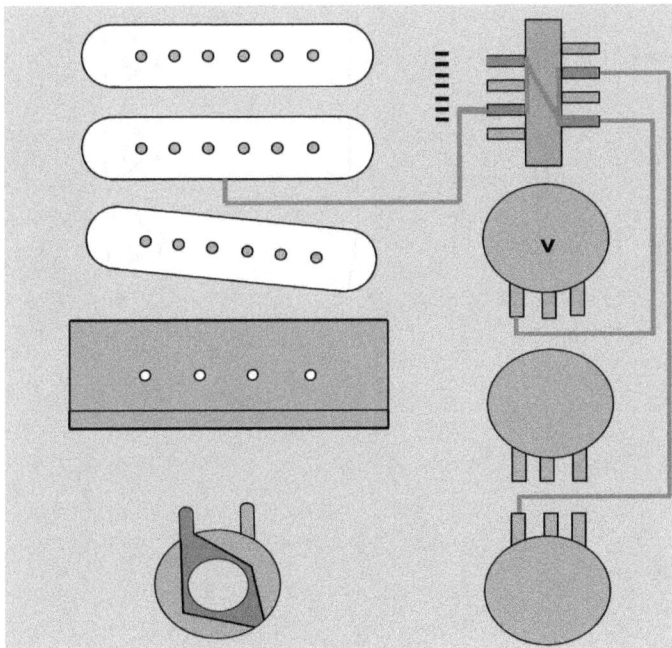

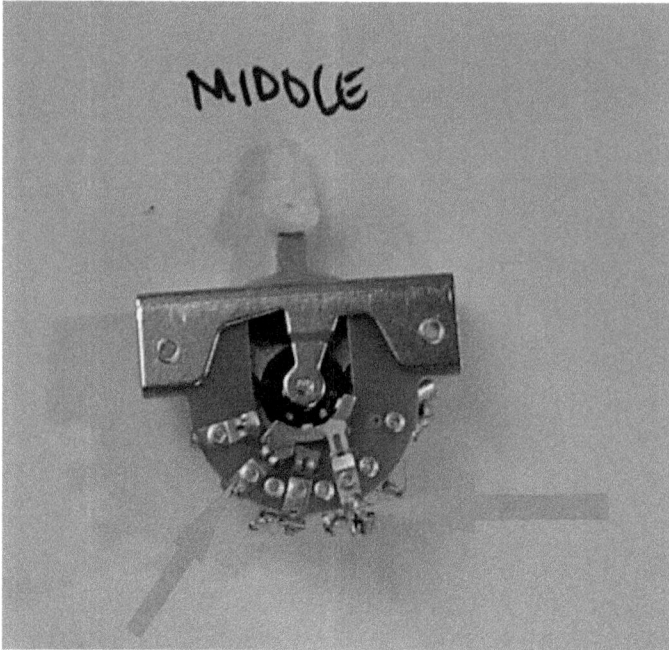

MIDDLE

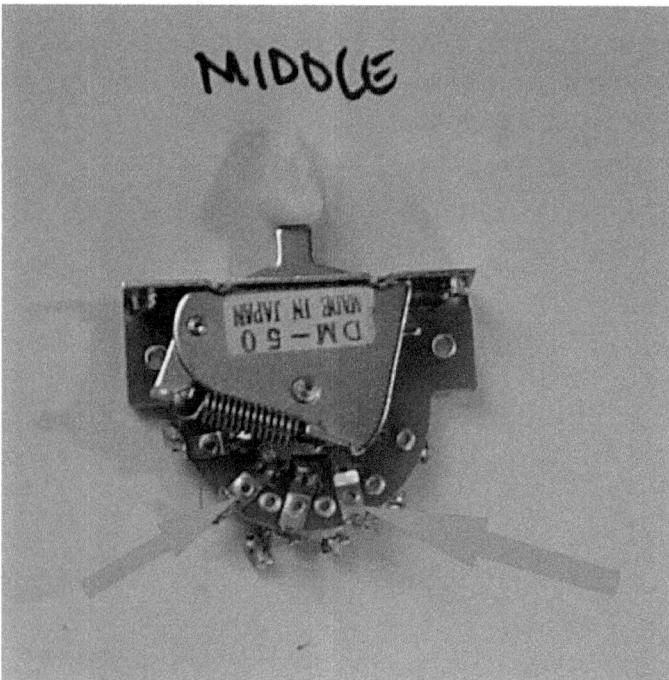

MIDDLE

The next selection is the middle and bridge pickups.

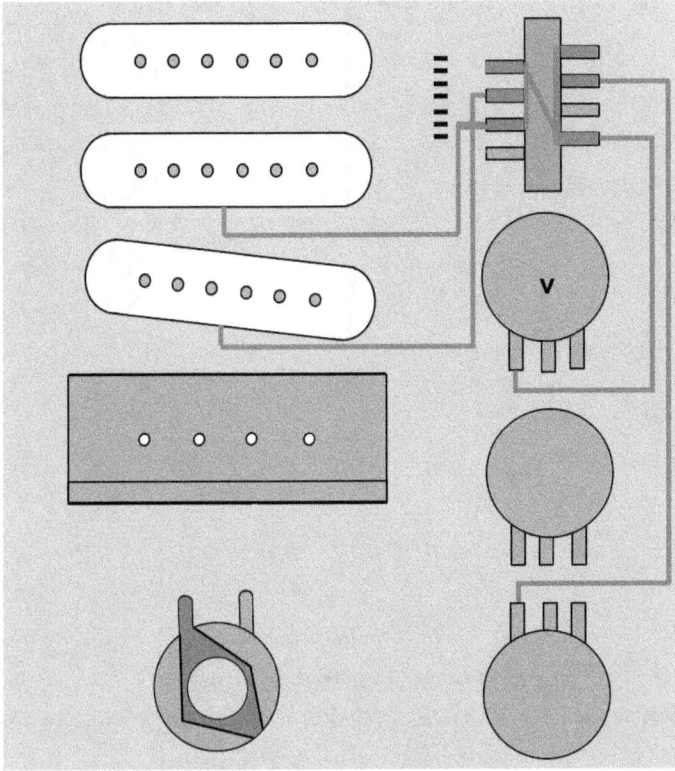

BRIDGE + MIDDLE

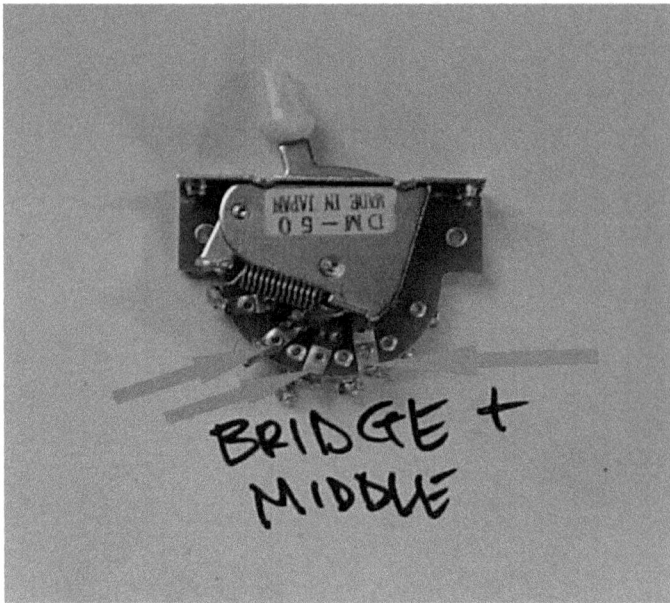

BRIDGE +
MIDDLE

The last choice is the bridge pickup selection. This choice offers alot of treble, and is perfect for playing heavy distortion and artificial harmonics. You can make the guitar scream with the bridge pickup. Notice there is no tone control for the bridge pickup. If you want more bass or midrange, then you need to select a different pickup, or modify your guitar.

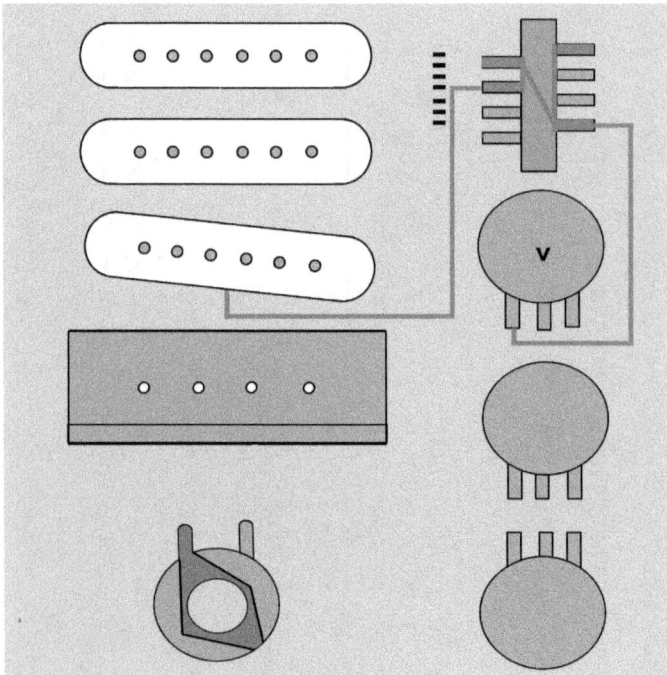

BRIDGE

BRIDGE

DM-50
MADE IN JAPAN

If you want to install a 5-way **mega switch** in your strat, then you can wire the guitar like this.

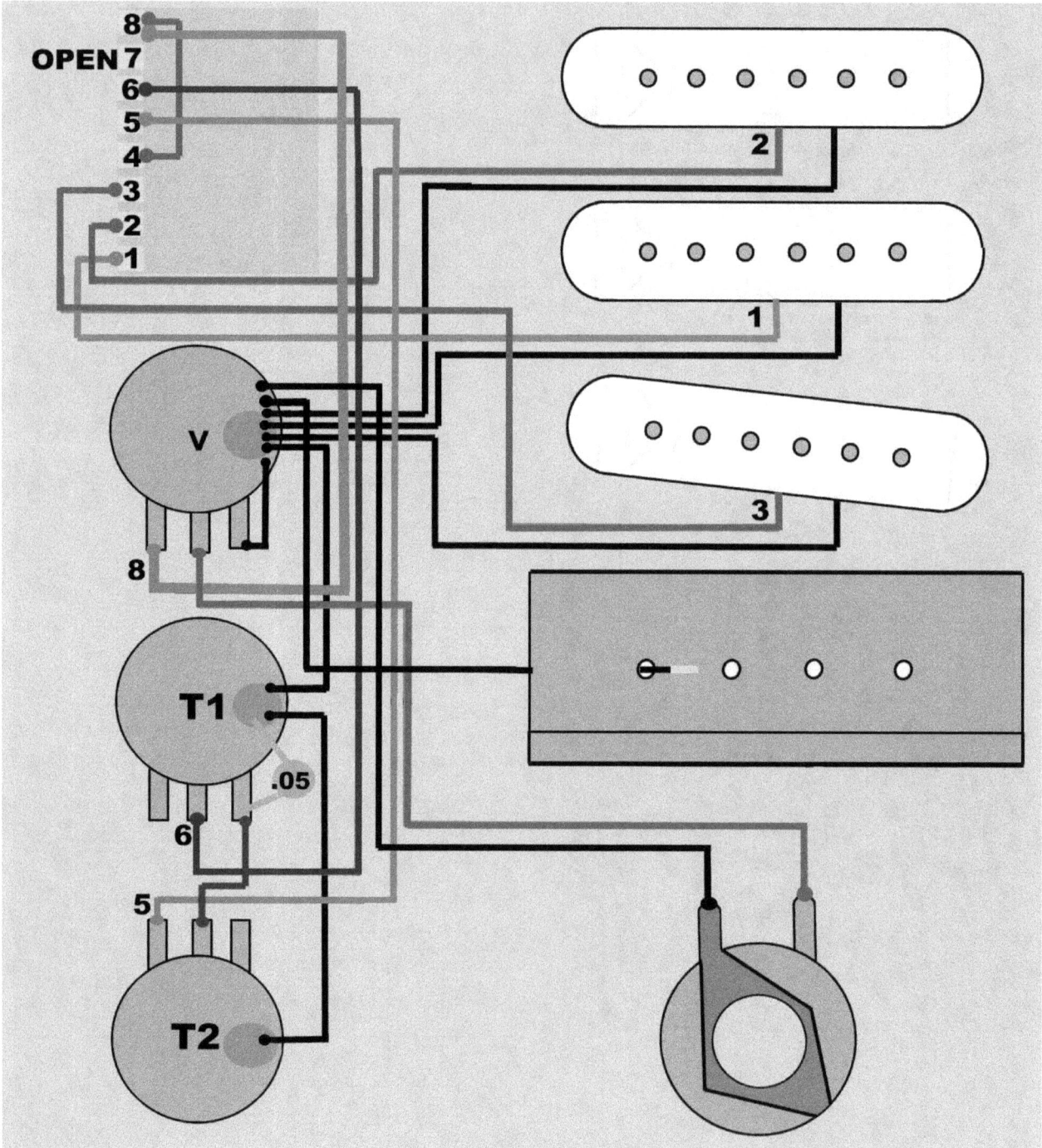

UNDERSTANDING TOGGLE SWITCHES

Toggle switches open or close a circuit. In other words, they turn a signal on or off. They can be used for all types of guitar modifications, including series/parallel wiring, phase reversal, and coil cutting. The mini toggle switches we will focus on in this book are **DPDT (double pole, double throw) switches.** Since they have 2 poles, they have two separate channels that are not connected to each other, unless you add a jumper wire.

MINI TOGGLE SWITCHES

POLE 1

POLE 2

This 2 way mini toggle switch below is an **on/on DPDT (double pole, double throw) switch,** and you can purchase them at www.stewmac.com for a little over $5. This switch is an on-on switch, meaning it turns one side on, or the other side on. So when one pickup is turned on, the other pickup is turned off. It has six lugs, 3 on the top, and 3 on the bottom. The lugs that are hot, or "on", are colored in blue or green. Each color represents a different pole.

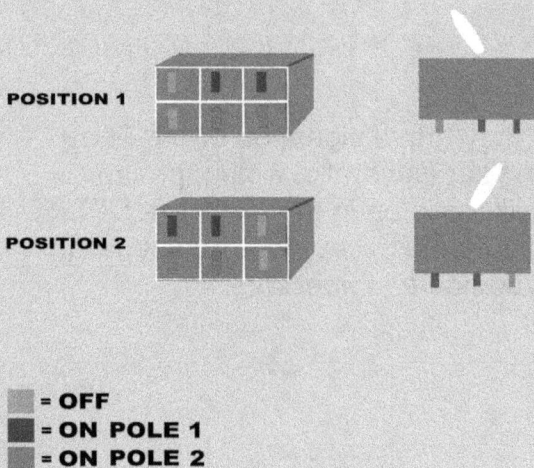

ON/ON SWITCH

POSITION 1

POSITION 2

= OFF
= ON POLE 1
= ON POLE 2

There are a few other types of 3-way mini toggle switches that can be useful in guitar wiring. One is a **on/off/on DPDT center-off switch.** It is the same as the on-on mini toggle switch with an additional stop in between the left and right setting. The middle position cuts the power. So it is an on-off-on switch. Here is what it looks like.

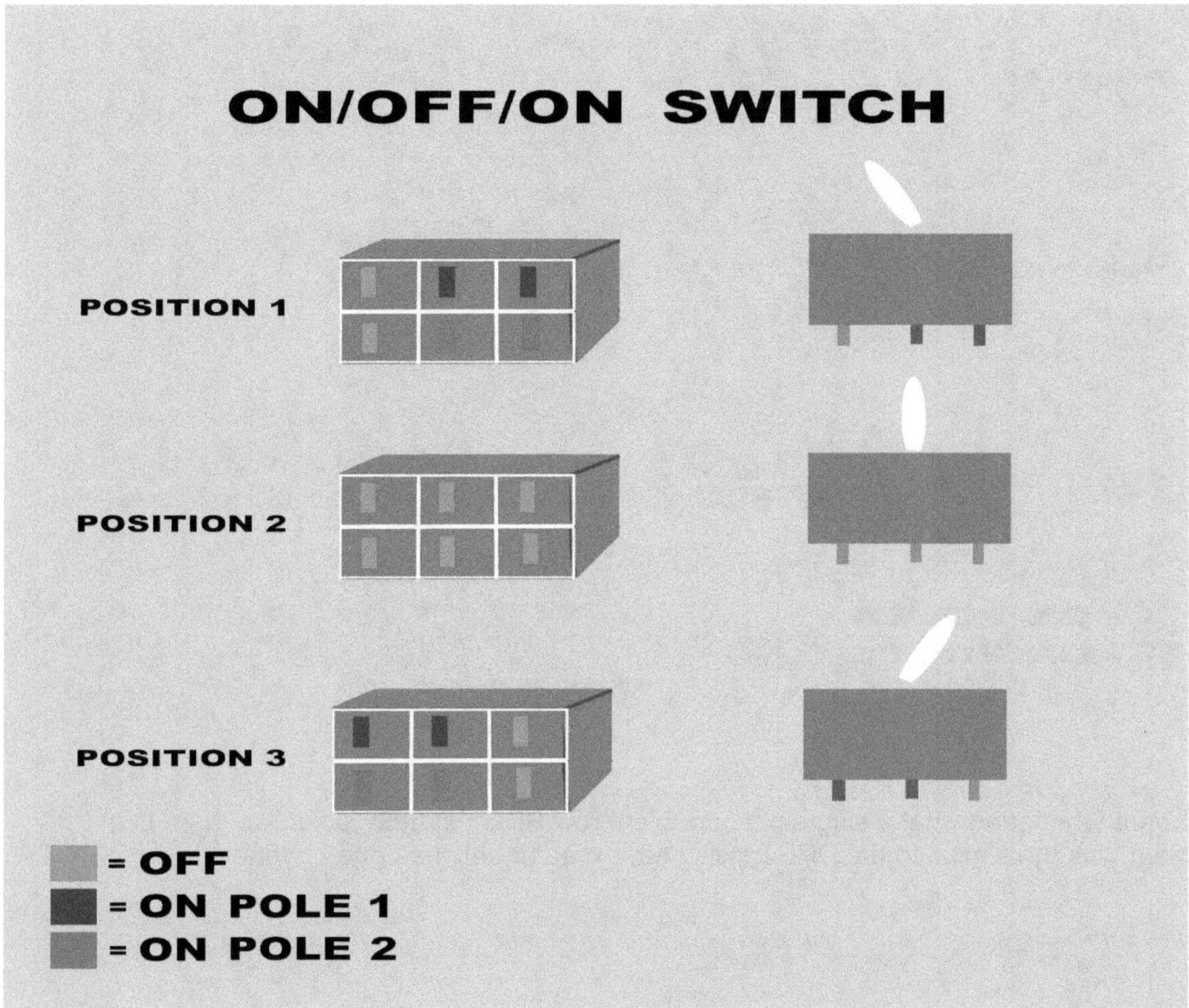

ON/OFF/ON SWITCH

POSITION 1

POSITION 2

POSITION 3

= OFF
= ON POLE 1
= ON POLE 2

The next 3 -way mini toggle switch is an **on/on/on DPDT center-on switch.** It is used for series/parallel switching, coil cutting, and phase reversing. It turns on the top left lugs and bottom right lugs while in the middle position.

- 53 -

ON/ON/ON SWITCH

POSITION 1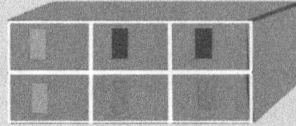

POSITION 2

POSITION 3

 = OFF
 = ON POLE 1
 = ON POLE 2

If you are wondering what a single pole double throw **SPDT switch** looks like, here is a diagram. It is the similar to the DPDT switches, except it only has one channel.

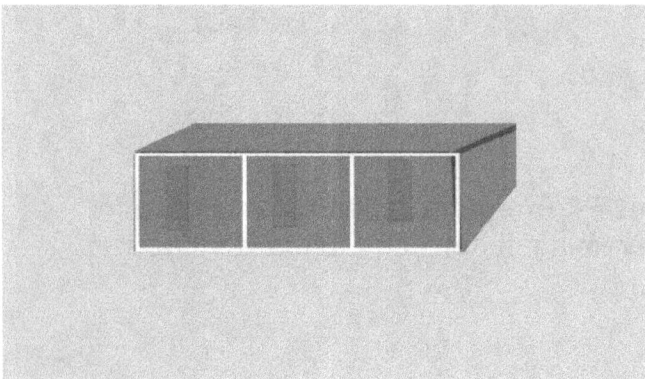

Here is the telecaster guitar wiring with two DPDT on-on toggle switches. Each toggle turns one pickup on or off.

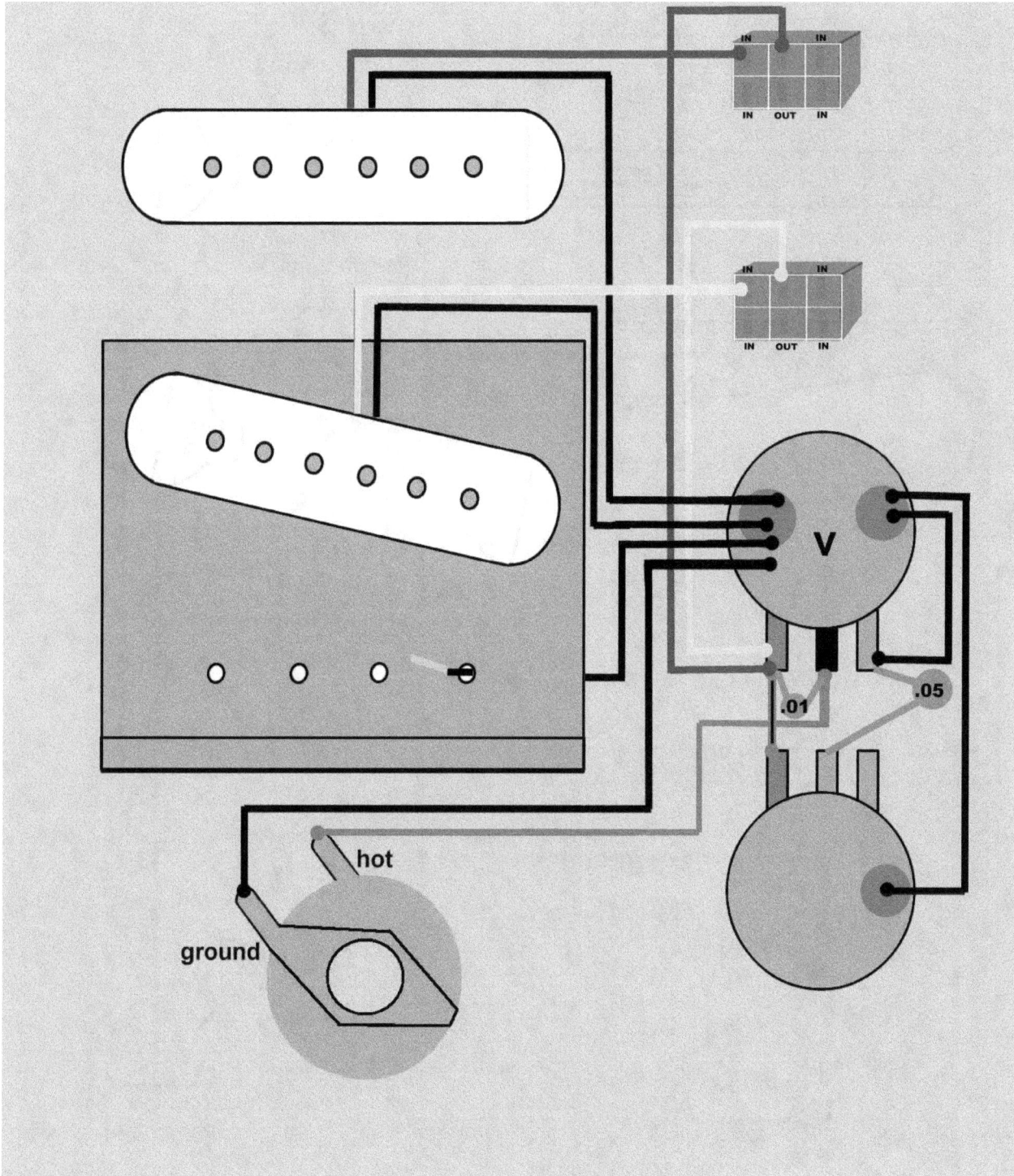

Next is the wiring for the strat with 3 toggle switches. Each one turns on a different pickup. You can get seven different tones with this setup.

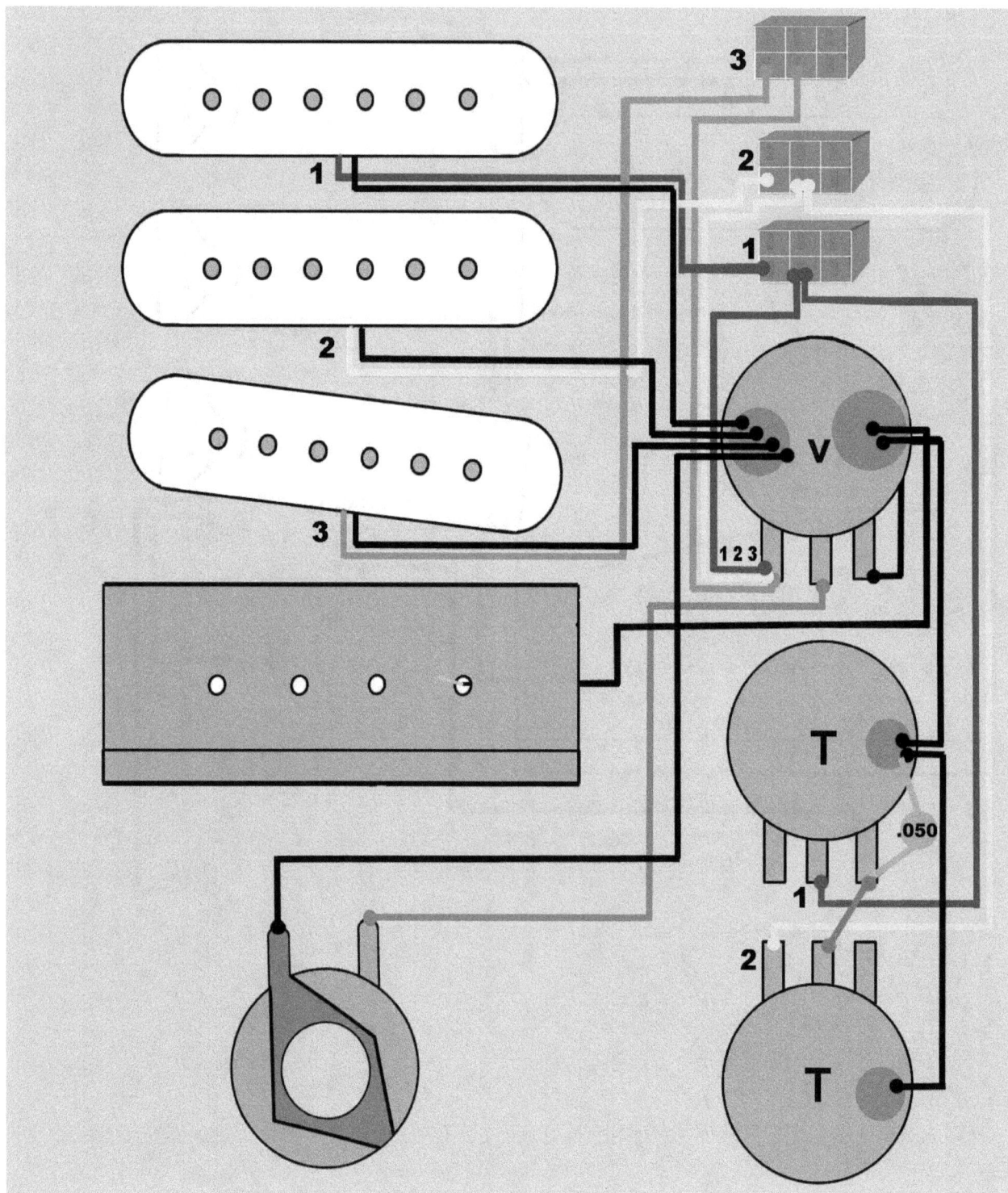

Not all toggles have 6 lugs. Some toggles have less. **Gibson style toggle switches**, for example, have 4 lugs and can turn on 2 separate devices at the same time (on, both on, on). Check out the Gibson style toggle below. Wiring them is fairly similar to the mini toggle. You have two inputs and two outputs. The ground wire gets soldered to the lug on the back. Solder the middle two output lugs together if you want both pickups on when the switch is in the middle position.

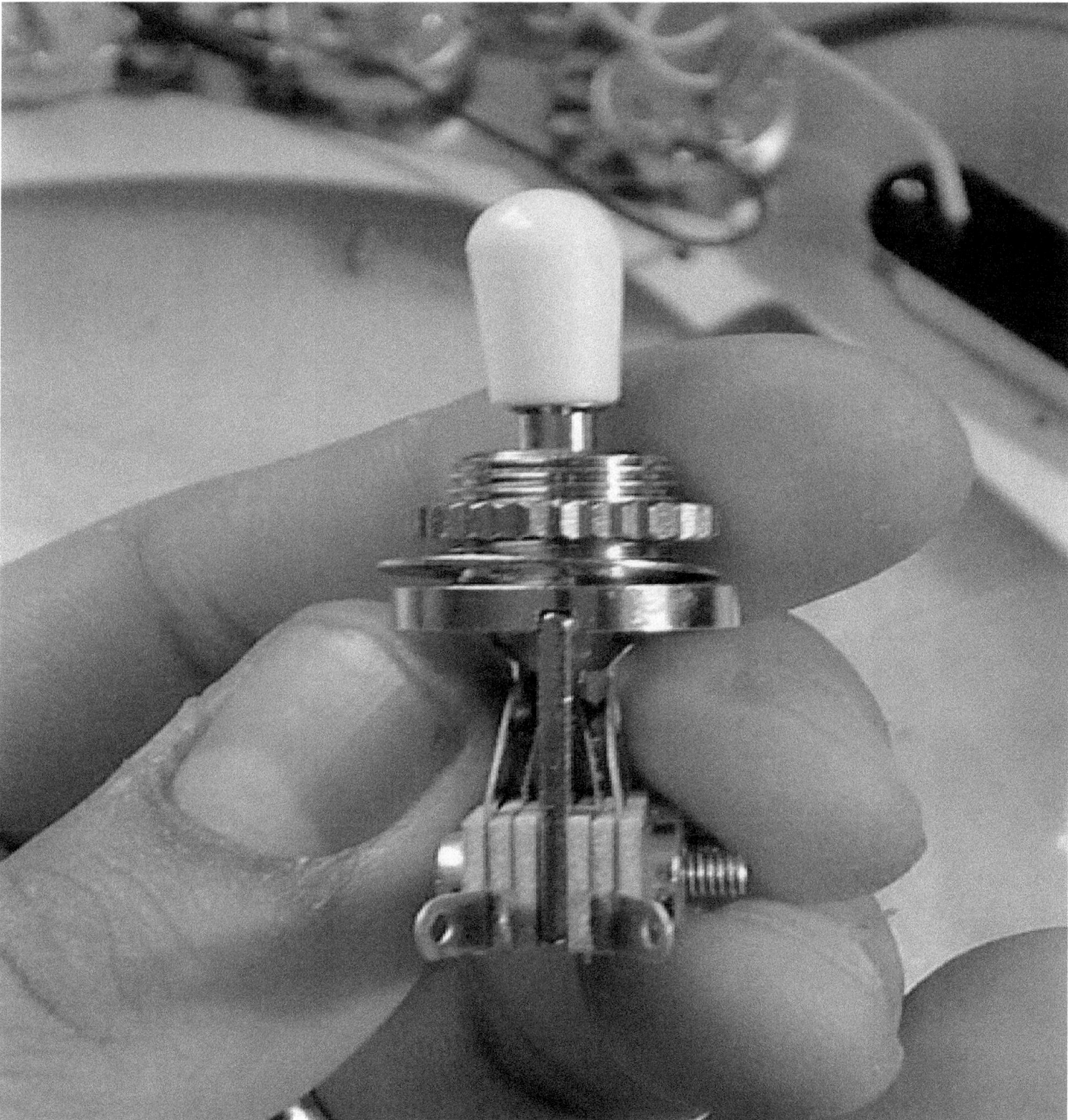

This next diagram will show you how the toggle works in the middle position. All lugs are touching, so both pickups are on.

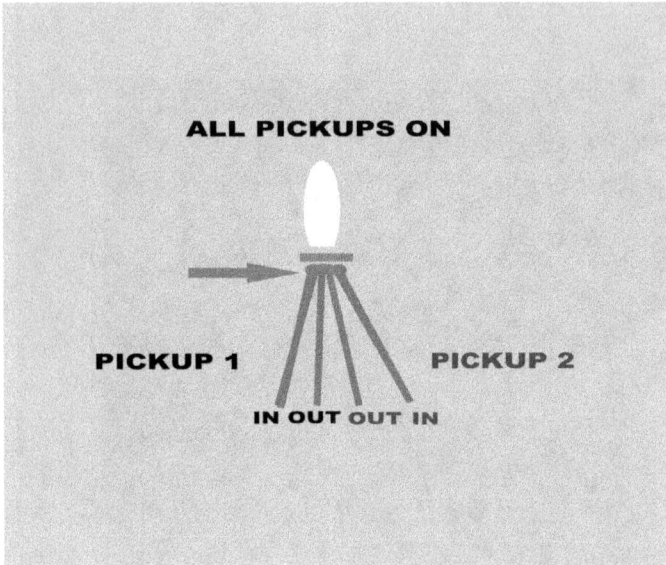

ALL PICKUPS ON

PICKUP 1   PICKUP 2

IN OUT OUT IN

In this next example, the right two lugs are touching, completing the circuit. One pickup is on, and the other is off.

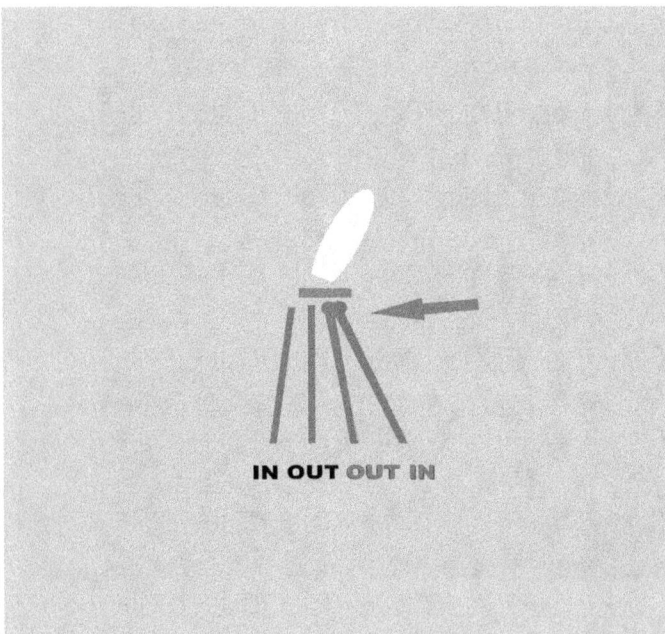

IN OUT OUT IN

This example shows what happens when the opposite side is turned on.

IN OUT OUT IN

Some Gibson style toggle switches only have three lugs, which is basically the same as the two middle output lugs being soldered together on a 4 lug toggle switch.

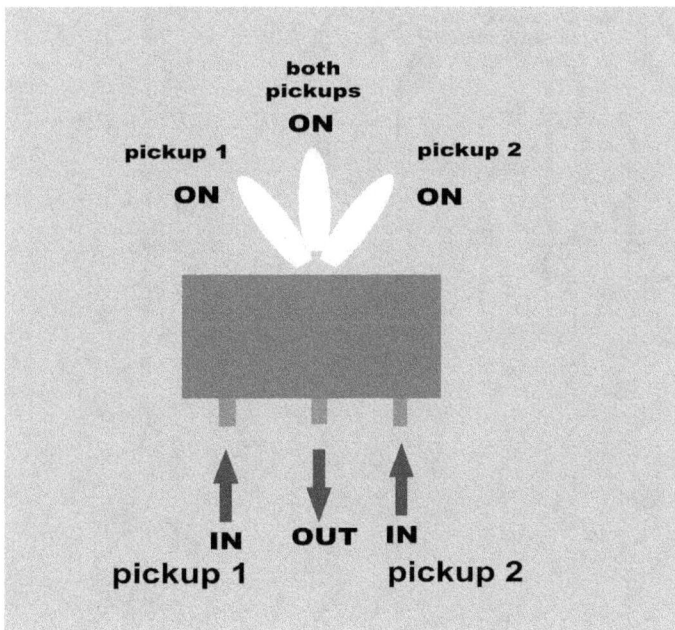

both
pickups
ON

pickup 1   pickup 2
ON   ON

IN   OUT   IN
pickup 1   pickup 2

The next page shows one way to wire a tele style guitar with a Gibson toggle. It would also work with any 2 pickup guitar that had one tone and one volume control. This way seems more practical than having a separate tone and volume knob for each pickup. But I guess that depends on how much time you want to spend changing settings while playing. This setup functions the same as a 3-way Fender style switch. You can turn on each pickup individually, or both at the same time. Also notice a ground wire is added to reduce unwanted noise.

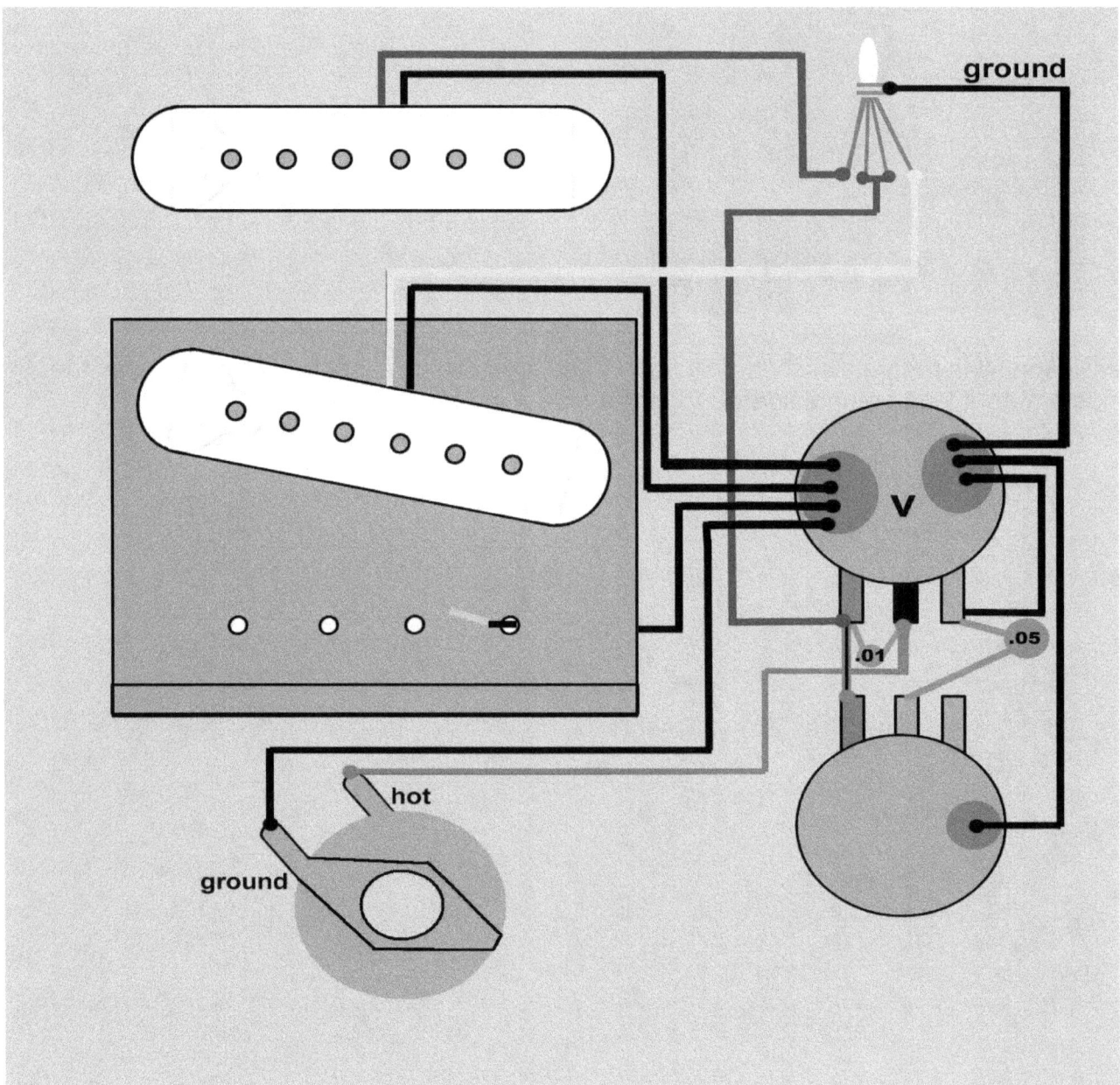

Here is the Les Paul with the Gibson toggle switch.

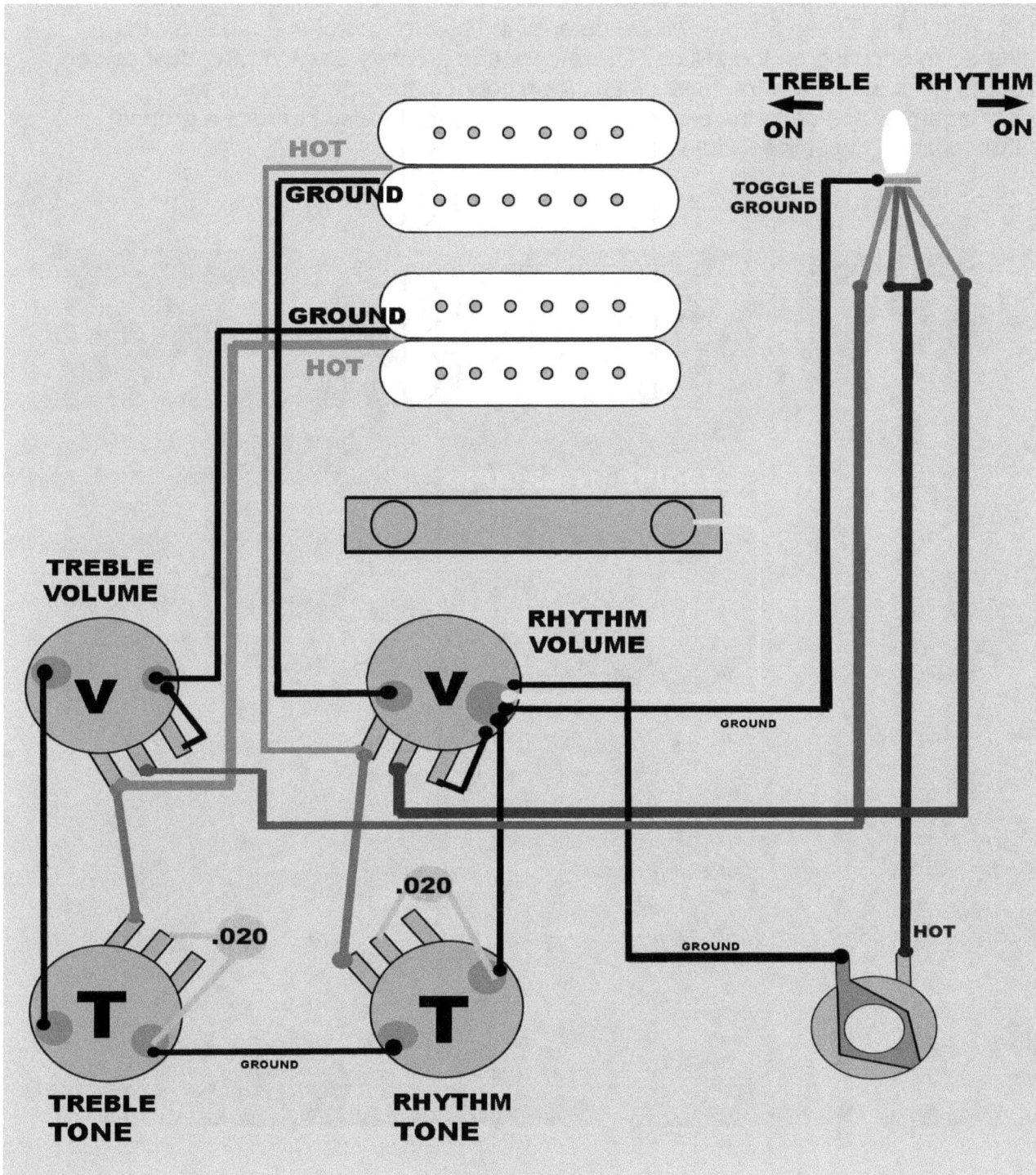

UNDERSTANDING VARITONE SWITCHES

The next switch we are going to discuss is the Varitone switch with the chicken head knob. This switch allows you to dial in specific tones for each setting, and eliminates any guesswork associated with the subtlety of tone potentiometers. This type of switch has 6 settings for 6 different tones. The first tone is usually clean, so that leaves 5 different tones to chose from. These 5 tones will be determined by the size of the capacitor that gets soldered to each lug on the switch. These switches are very easy to wire. Just solder capacitors to each lug on the Varitone switch, then connect the open ends of the capacitors together, and send the signal out to the output jack. Also connect a ground wire to the common lug in the middle of the switch.

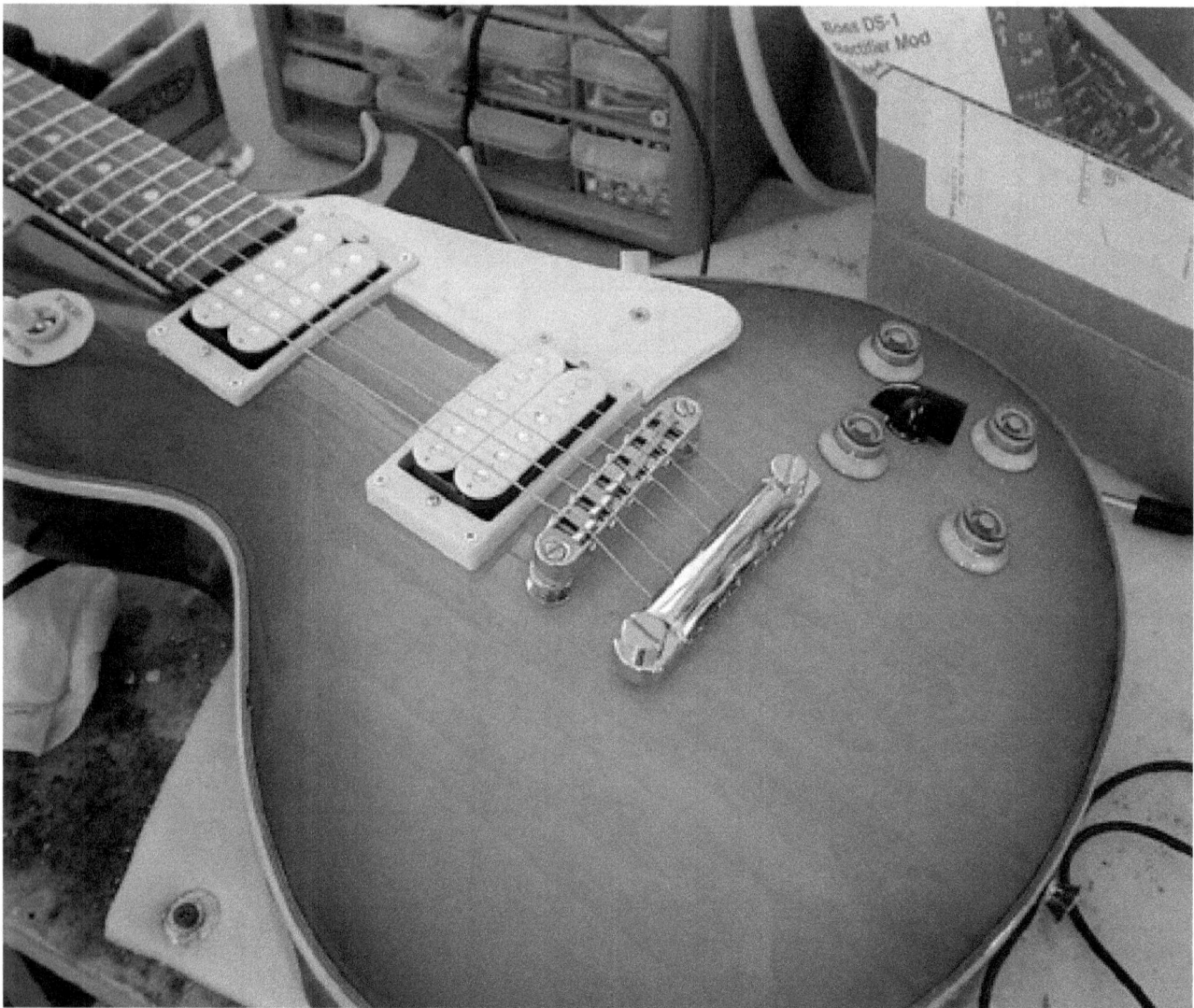

Below are some capacitor values used on the Gibson 345 Lucille guitar. These values are measured in microfarads. The bigger capacitors will give you a muddier sound. You can experiment to find the tones you want by using different capacitor values.

LUG 6 - 0.22 µF
LUG 5 - 0.03 µF
LUG 4 - 0.01 µF
LUG 3 - 0.003 µF
LUG 2 - 0.001 µF
LUG 1 - no capacitor (clean sound)

Here is how you install a Varitone in a Les Paul style guitar. First, drill a hole in the body. Then install the Varitone switch. Mark on the switch the lugs that you will be using. When you look at the side of the switch, you can see which lug is in use. This particular switch has 12 lugs which can be used for additional functions. We will only be soldering capacitors to 5 of these lugs, so turn the switch through all 6 positions, and notice which lug is completing the circuit at each setting. Then you will know which 5 lugs need to have capacitors soldered to them. One out of those 6 settings is left open, so it gets a clean, unaltered sound.

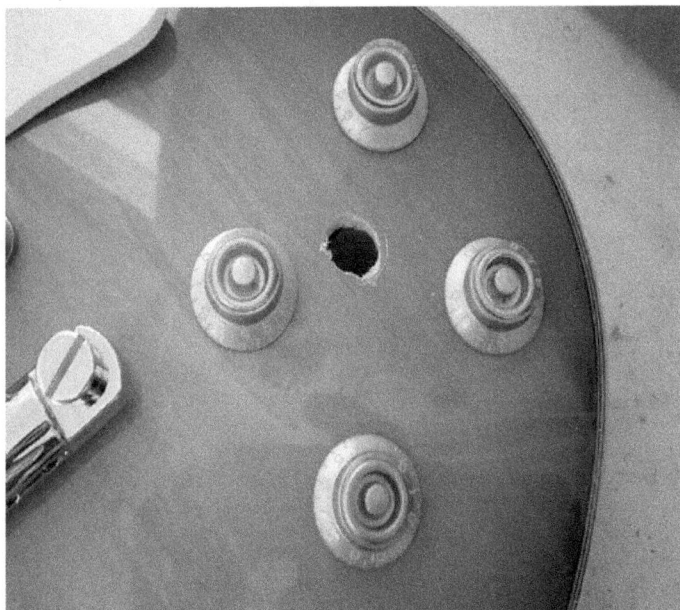

Here are the lugs that we will be using.

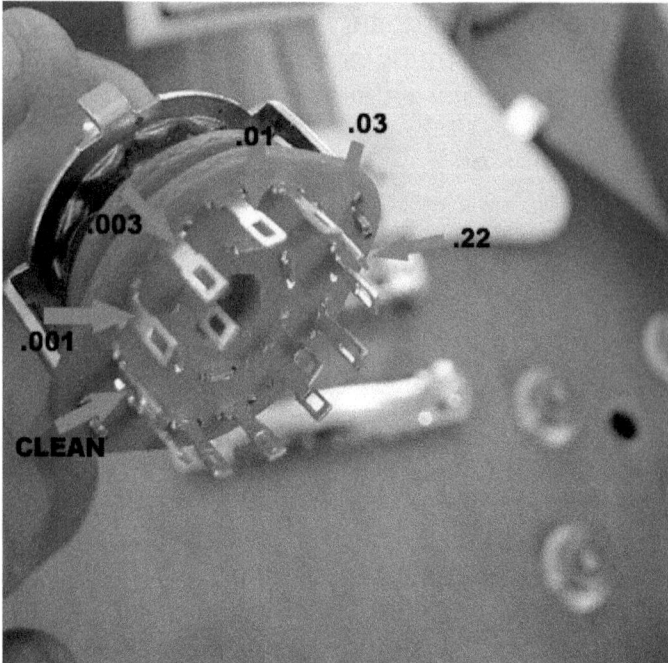

Here are the capacitors that I chose for this project.

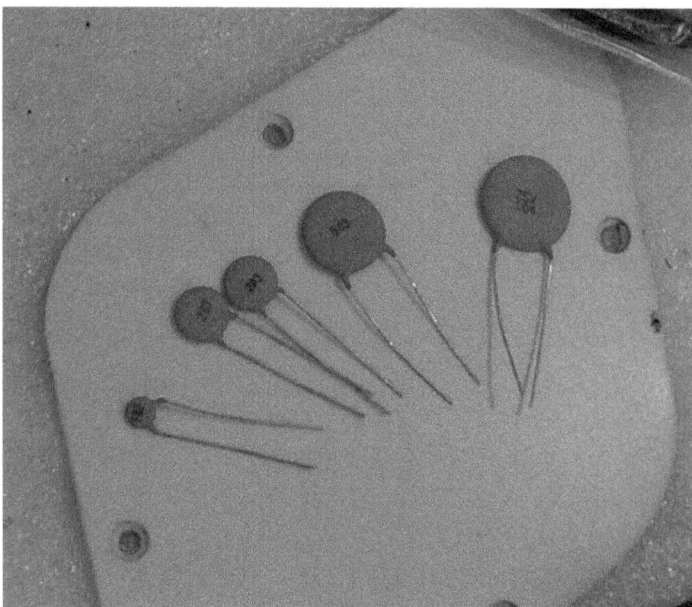

Now solder one end of each capacitor to one of the lugs on the Varitone switch. Solder them in ascending order.

- 64 -

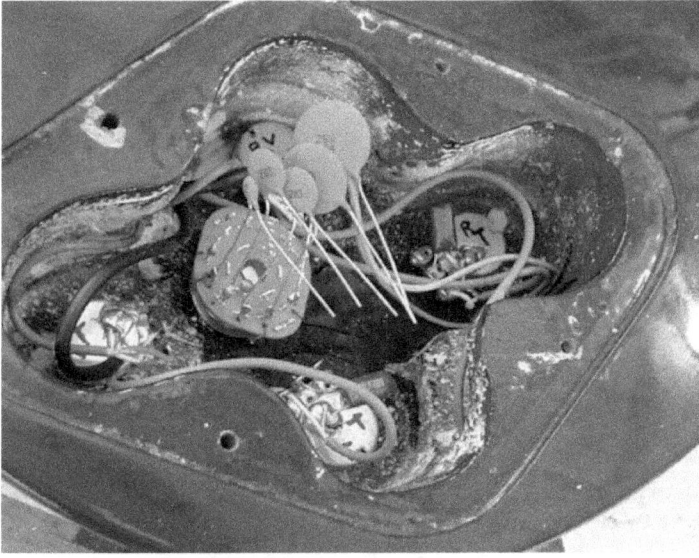

Now solder all of the open ends of the capacitors together. These will be soldered to a wire that connects to the hot lug on the output jack.

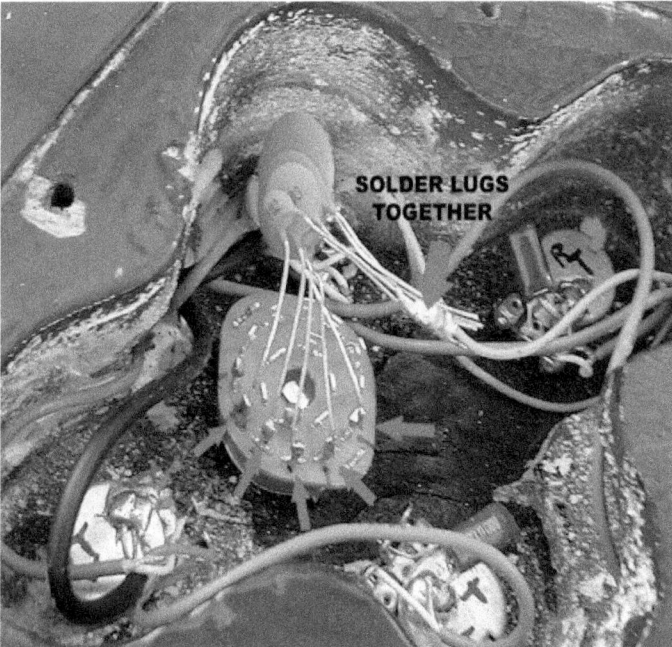

SOLDER LUGS TOGETHER

Solder the ground wire. It attaches to the common lug in the middle of the Varitone switch, closest to the lugs you just soldered. From there, it gets soldered to the bottom of one of the volume or tone pots. In other words, it gets connected to ground.

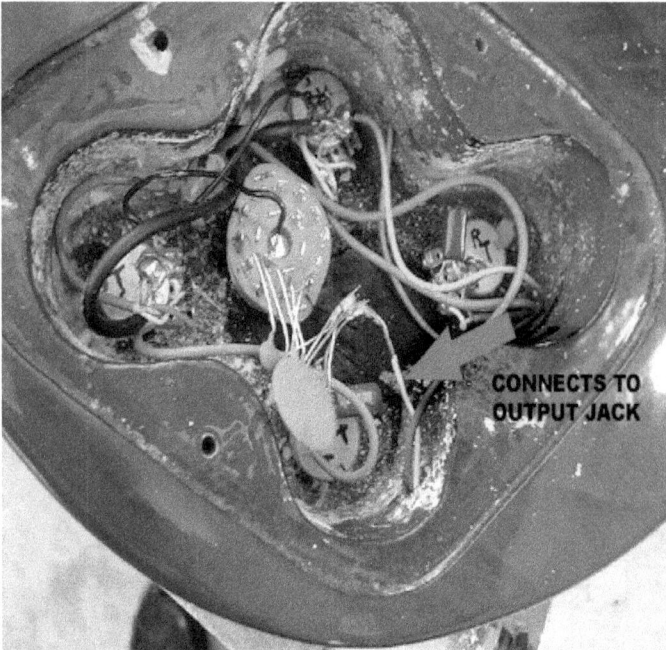

CONNECTS TO
OUTPUT JACK

Here is the output jack with two wires connected to the hot lug.

HOT WIRE FROM
TOGGLE SWITCH

GROUND WIRE

HOT WIRE FROM
VARITONE SWITCH

Here is the finished wiring.

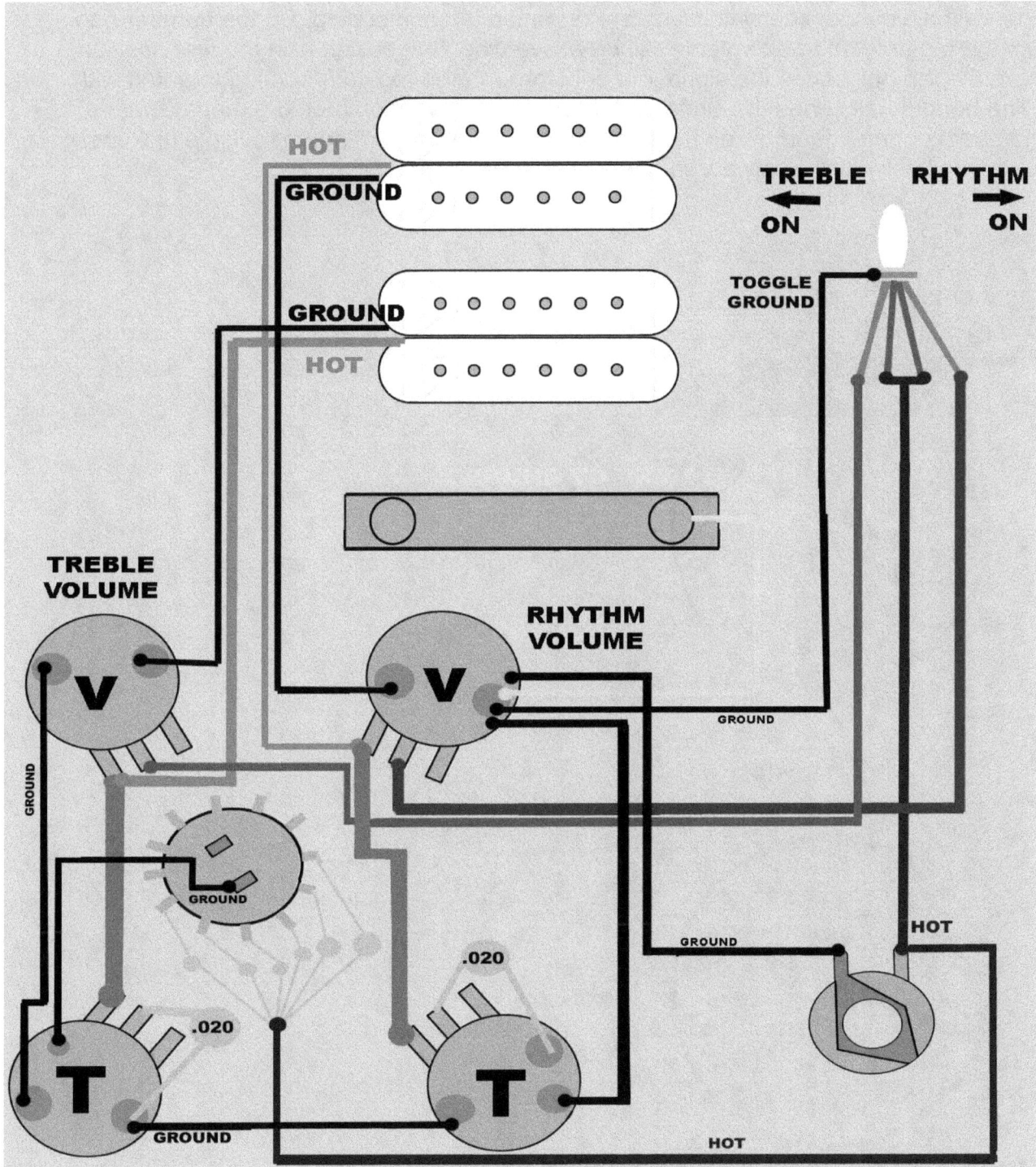

You could also use the Varitone switch to replace your existing 3 or 5-way switch. Rotary switches, like the Varitone, are very similar to lever switches. However, each side, or pole, only turns on one lug at a time. Some of the selections on 5-way switches turn on several lugs. In the diagram below, the switch is in position one. If you look closely at the Varitone switch, you can see which lugs are engaged in each setting. So the number one lug from the top pole and bottom pole will be active when the switch is in the first position. However, the top half sends the signal out only through the top common lug, marked with a "c". The bottom half sends the signal out through the lower common lug marked with a "c". A jumper is often added to link the two sides together for turning on multiple pickups. The diagrams below show how a Varitone works in each position.

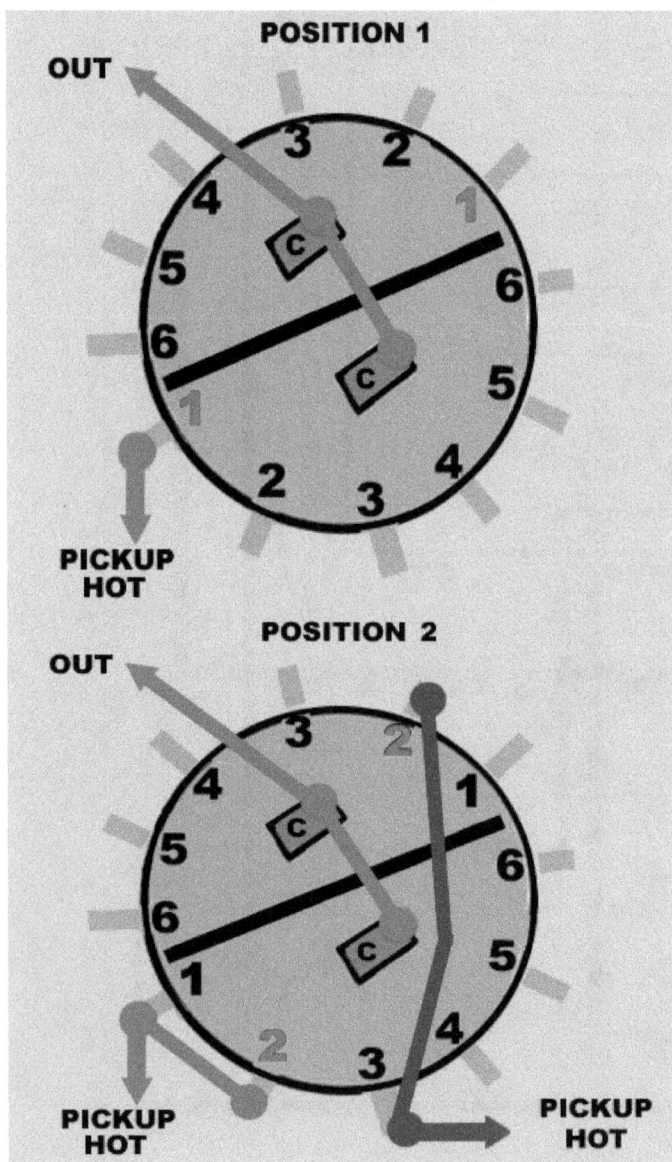

POSITION 1

OUT

PICKUP
HOT

POSITION 2

OUT

PICKUP
HOT

PICKUP
HOT

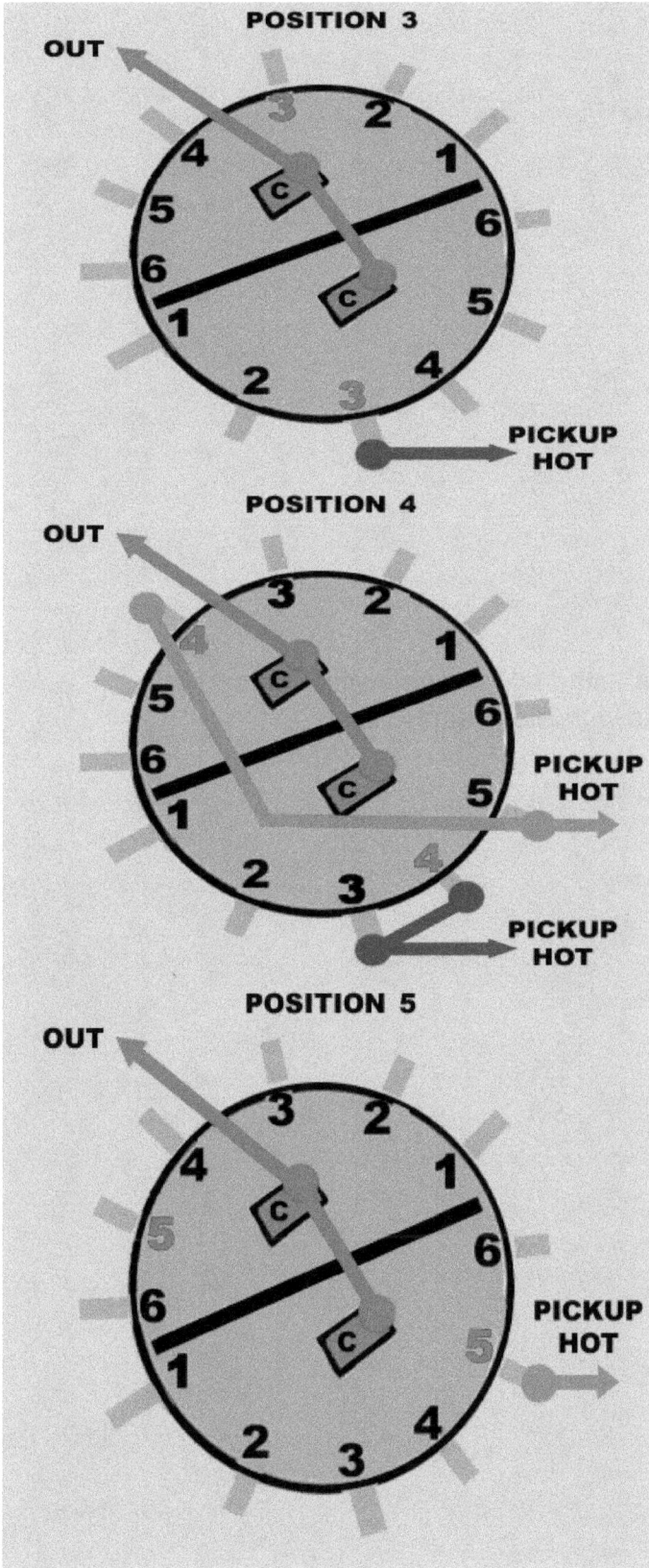

POSITION 3

POSITION 4

POSITION 5

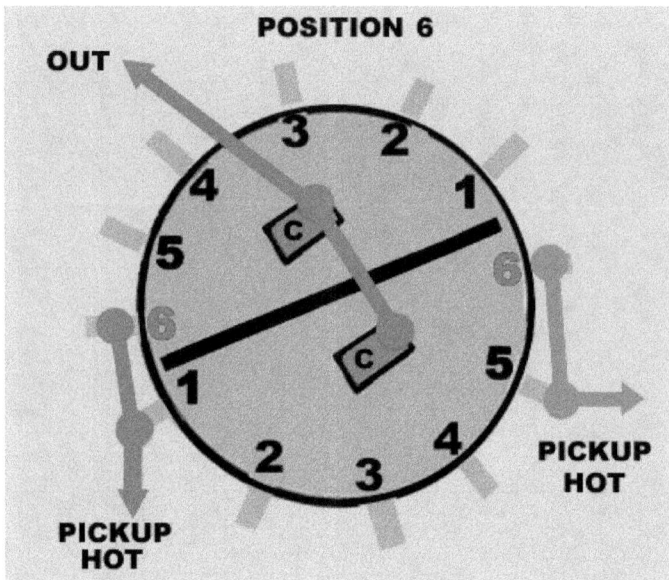

POSITION 6

The next page shows a wiring diagram for a strat using a Varitone switch instead of a lever switch. Notice you get six different positions with the Varitone switch.

position 1 = neck

position 2 = neck and middle

position 3 = middle

position 4 = middle and bridge

position 5 = bridge

position 6 = neck and bridge

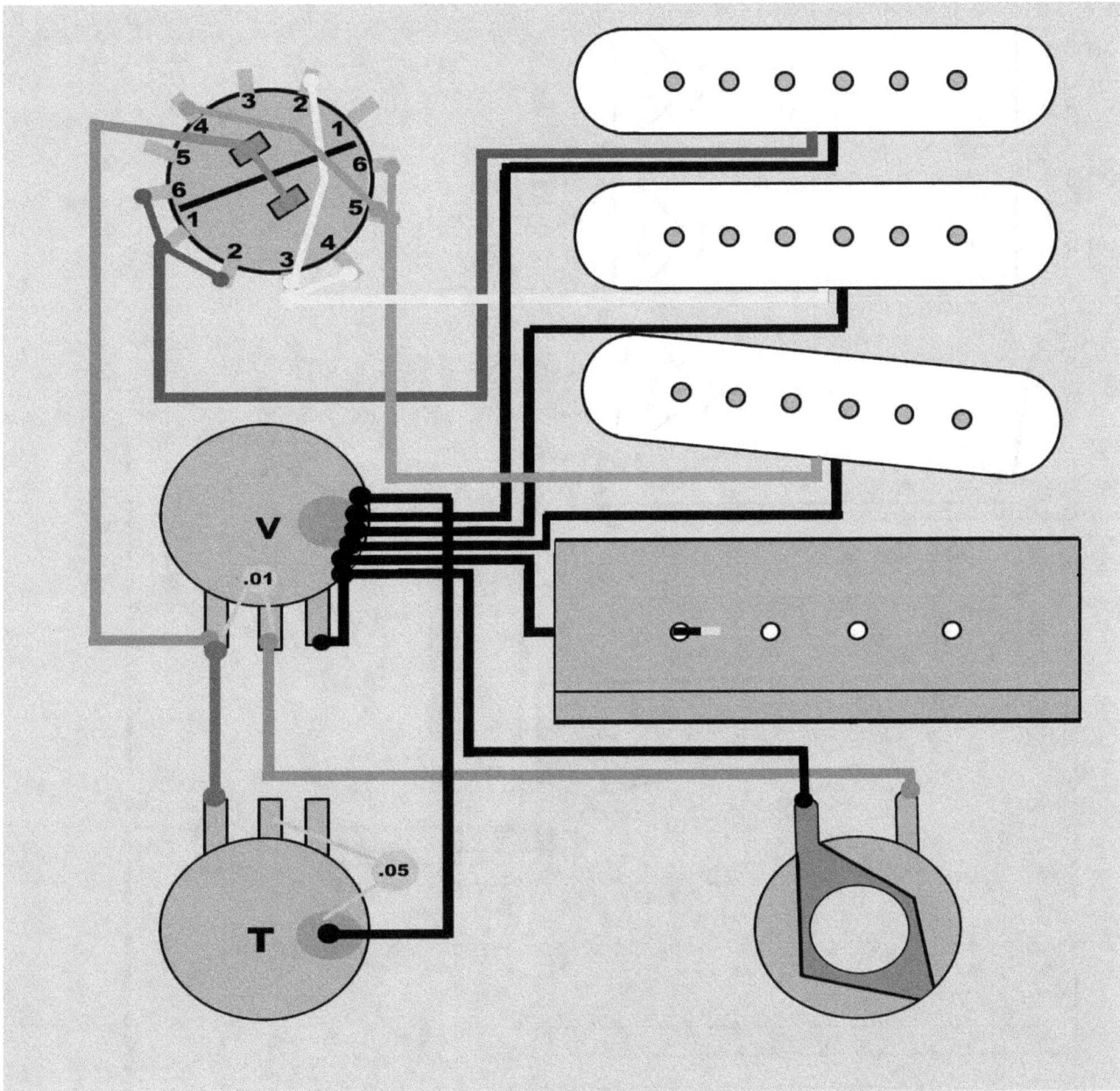

If you have a tele, or two pickup guitar, then you will have 3 additional positions that you can use if you want to. In the next diagram, capacitors are soldered to the lugs on the top half of the switch and then exit to ground. This setup will turn on the bridge pickup and a capacitor in positions 4, 5, and 6. The bigger the capacitor, the more bass your guitar will have.

position 1 = neck

position 2 = neck and bridge

position 3 = bridge

position 4 = bridge and capacitor .001

position 5 = bridge and capacitor .02

position 6 = bridge and capacitor .05

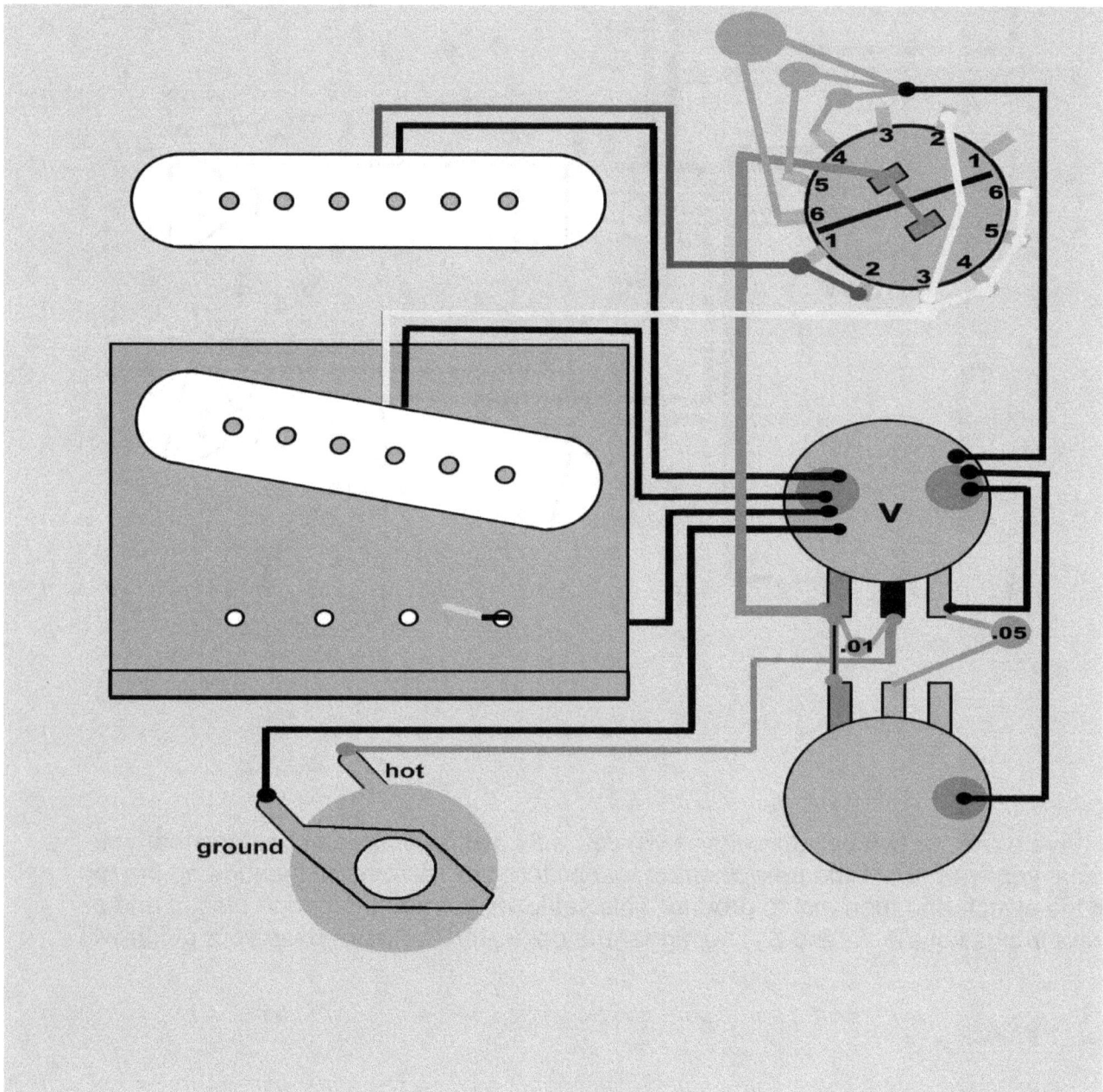

YAMAHA SWITCHES

One of the more complicated switches that you can use is called a Yamaha switch. It has 4 different poles, or channels. And each pole has 6 lugs. This allows for an unlimited range of wiring designs. The hot lugs are colored in red. The white dots show you where the lever is located at in each position.

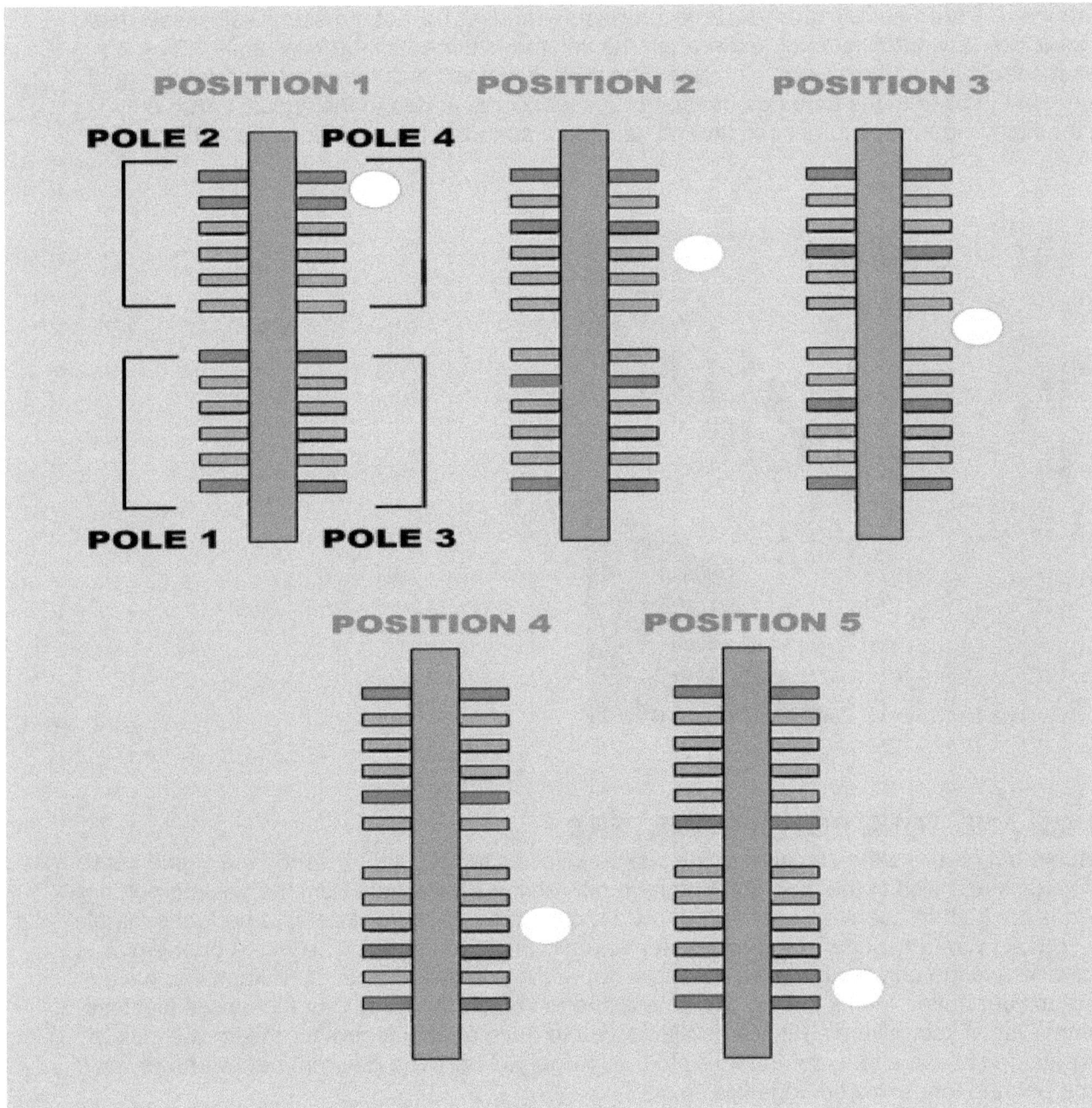

UNDERSTANDING POTENTIOMETERS

A potentiometer, commonly referred to as a pot, is a variable DC resistor. Basically, it decreases the signal that is going through it. As you decrease the signal in your volume or tone pot, you increase the signal that gets sent to ground. So if you have your volume set at 0, 100% of the signal will be sent to ground. Normally 250K Ohm pots are used with single coil pickups to add warmth to the sound, and 500K Ohm pots are used with humbucking pickups to add more highs to the sound. A 1 Meg pot will give you an even brighter sound. Part of the signal will always leak out to ground in any potentiometer, even when the volume is turned all the way up. A 1 Meg pot will leak the least amount of signal to ground, and a 250K pot will leak the most amount of signal to ground. In the case of the tone potentiometer, a capacitor is added to the circuit, which only allows the high frequencies to pass to ground, leaving a sound with more midrange and bass.

VOLUME AND TONE POTENTIOMETERS
The volume pot receives the signal from the pickup selector switch. It then sends the signal out to the output jack and also to the tone pot. The tone pot receives the signal from the volume pot, and then sends the high frequencies out to ground via a capacitor. The telecaster is a perfect example of how you can wire any guitar with one master volume and tone control. The wiring on the pickup selector switch is the only thing that will change, depending on the number of pickups you have installed on your guitar. I think having one tone and one volume for all of your pickups is alot less confusing. Plus, if you have a strat, it also allows you to have a tone control for the bridge pickup. (Most strats don't have a tone control wired to the bridge pickup.) The diagram below shows how a volume pot and tone pot work together.

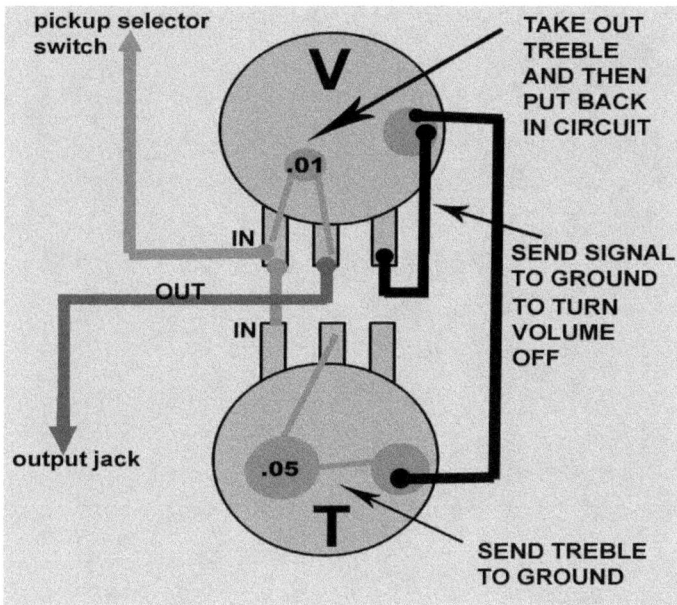

pickup selector switch

V

.01

IN

OUT

IN

output jack

.05

T

TAKE OUT TREBLE AND THEN PUT BACK IN CIRCUIT

SEND SIGNAL TO GROUND TO TURN VOLUME OFF

SEND TREBLE TO GROUND

BLEND POTENTIOMETERS

A blend pot, or stacked concentric pot, is a potentiometer that controls two pickups. Its a unique substitute for a pickup selector switch. However, it doesn't just turn on a pickup like a switch does. It can turn on a percentage of a pickup's volume. Basically, one direction increases the volume of pickup A, while decreasing the volume of pickup B. Turn the knob in the opposite direction, and it increases the volume of pickup B, and decreases the volume of pickup A. In the middle position, both pickups are at 100% volume. A mini toggle switch can be added to turn on the bridge pickup when wiring a strat.

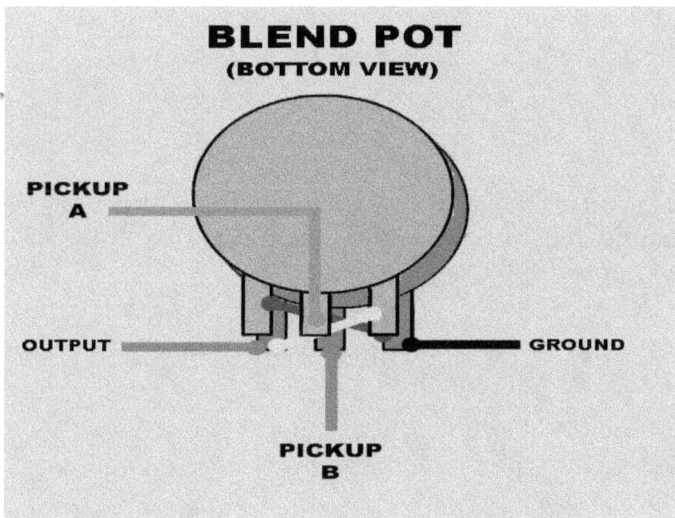

BLEND POT
(BOTTOM VIEW)

PICKUP A

OUTPUT

GROUND

PICKUP B

BLEND POT
(SIDE VIEW)

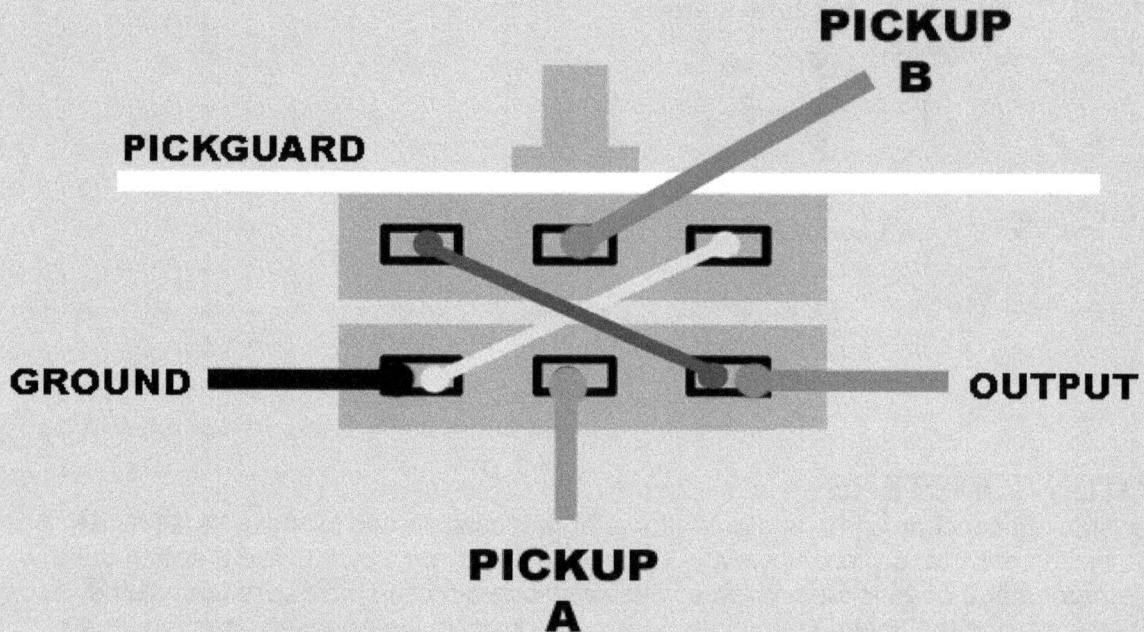

PICKUP B

PICKGUARD

GROUND

OUTPUT

PICKUP A

On the next page is a tele style wiring with a blend pot. You will have to drill a hole in the control plate to add this pot because there is still a master volume in the control plate. If you don't want a master volume control, you can always install the blend pot where the volume pot was.

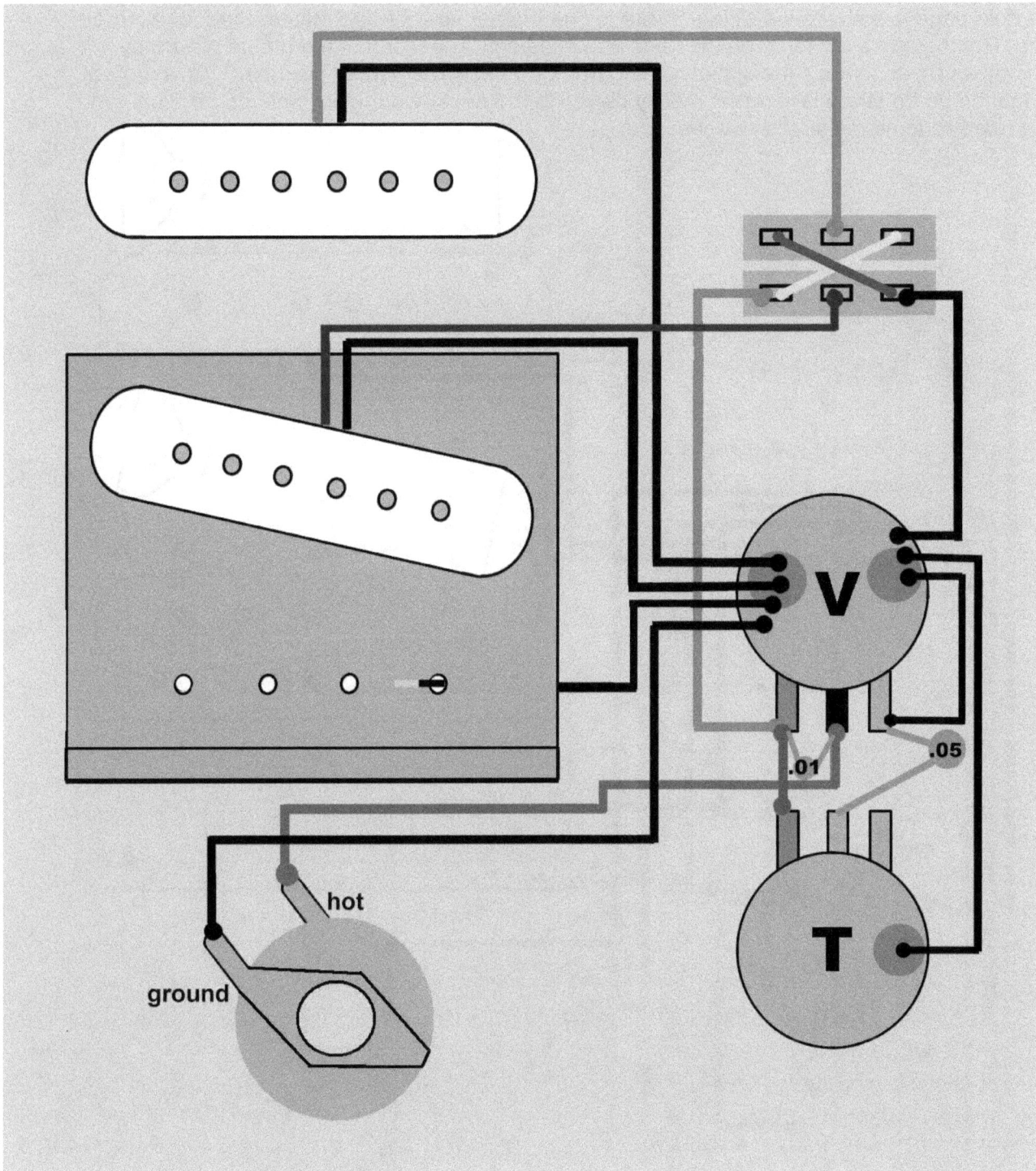

hot

ground

.01

.05

V

T

On the next page is a strat style wiring. There is one master volume and master tone for all three pickups. The toggle switch turns on the neck and middle pickups, or just the bridge pickup by itself. The blend pot controls the signal coming from the neck and middle pickups. This is a great wiring technique for strat players that mainly play with the neck and middle pickups on. That tone is often referred to as the strat's sweet sound.

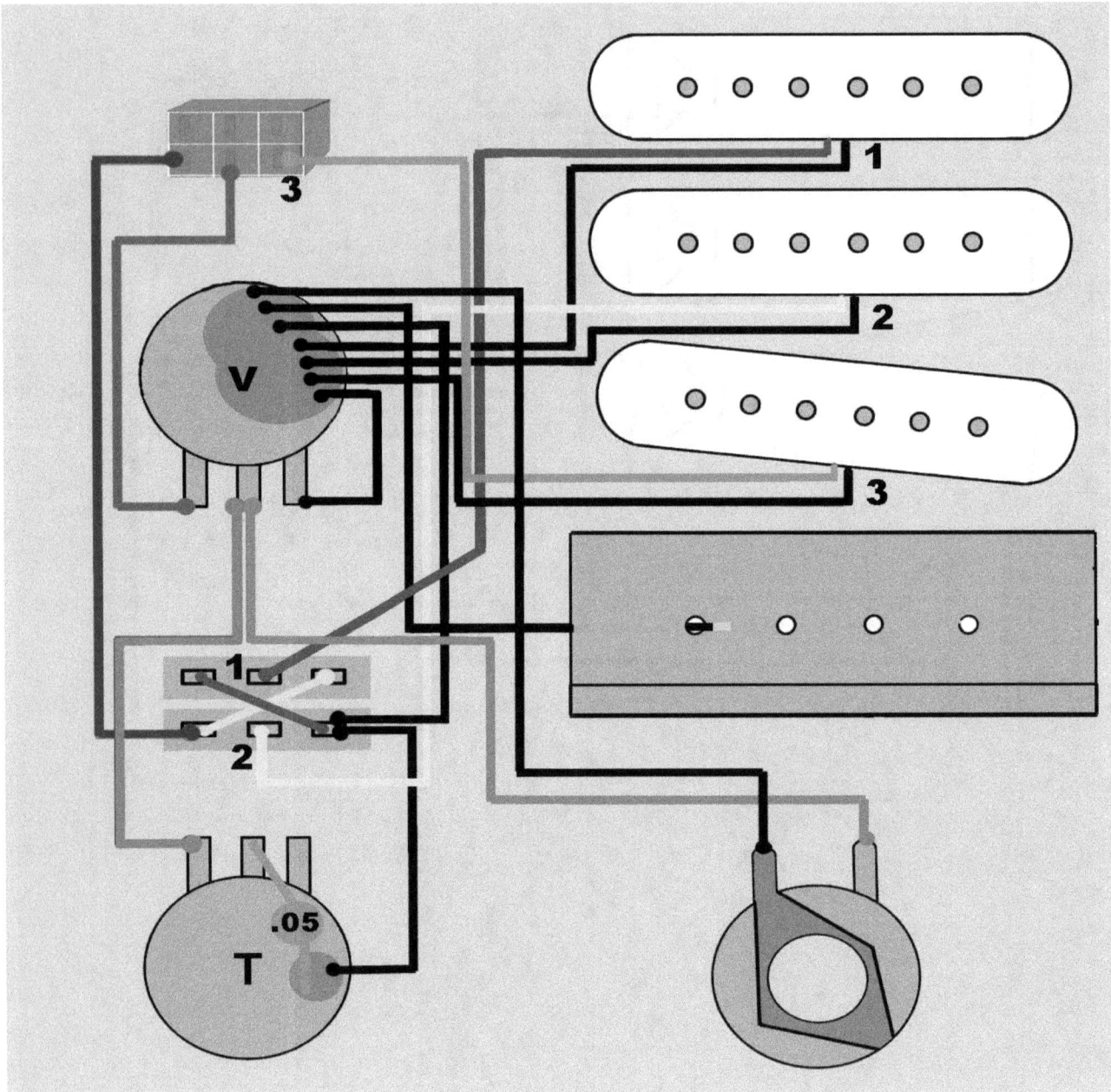

PUSH PULL POTENTIOMETERS

A push pull potentiometer is basically a combination of a DPDT on-on mini toggle switch and a potentiometer. This type of pot is designed to conserve space inside your guitar. Otherwise, you would need to drill a hole in your pickguard to add a mini toggle switch. Think of it like a separate potentiometer, and a separate DPDT mini toggle switch stuck together. When the knob is in the up position, it turns on the top 4 lugs. Note: there are two poles, or channels in each push pull pot switch. So the green lugs and the blue lugs are on, but they are not connected to each other. For more info on DPDT switches, check out the section on switches.

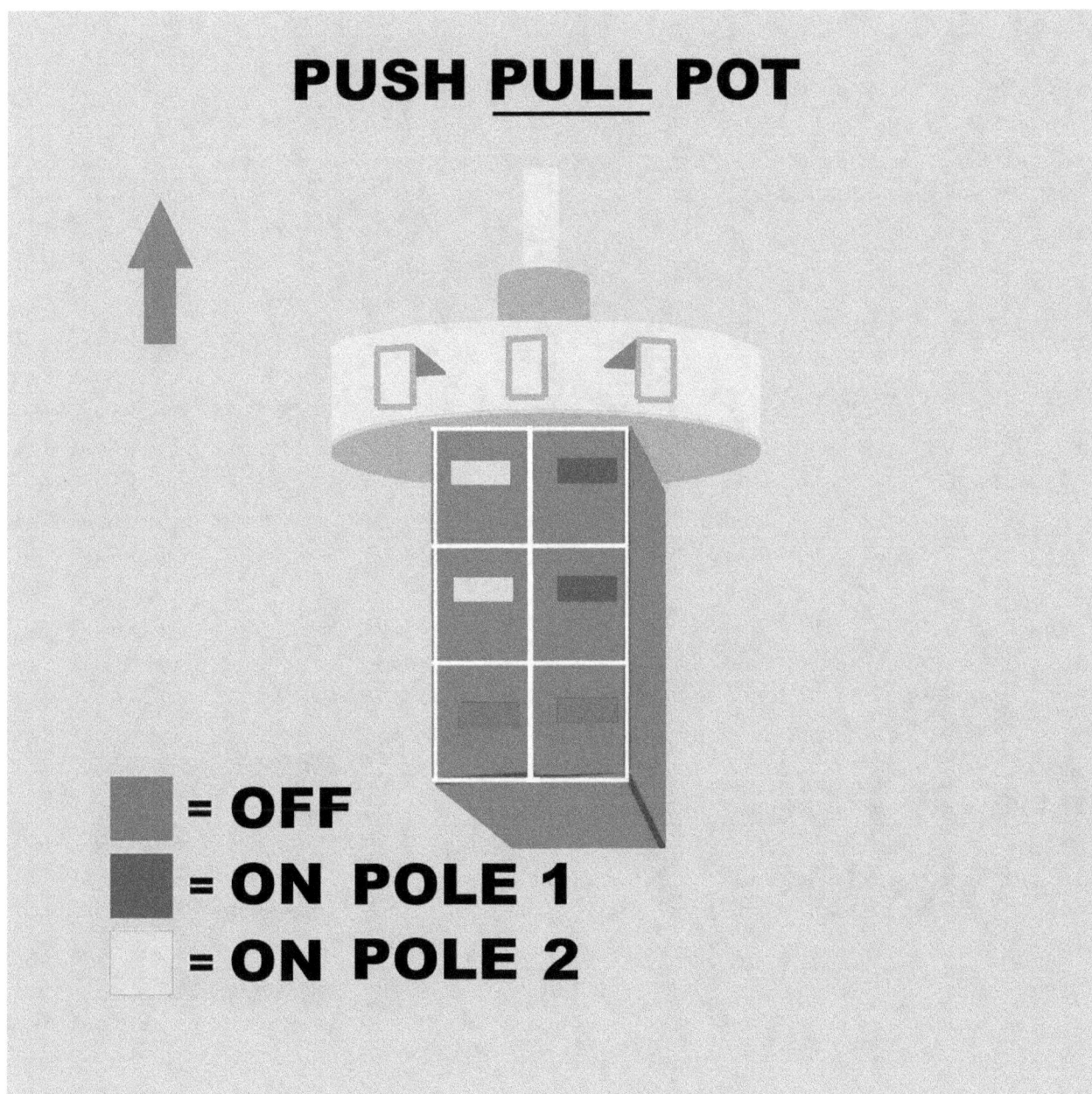

PUSH PULL POT

= OFF

= ON POLE 1

= ON POLE 2

When the knob is in the down position, it turns on the bottom 4 lugs.

PUSH PULL POT

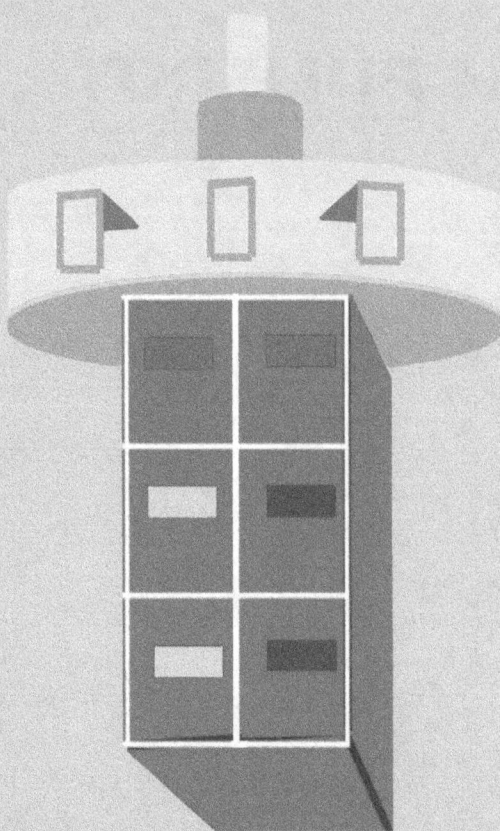

■ = OFF

■ = ON POLE 1

□ = ON POLE 2

Next is an example of a push pull pot that is being used as a tone pot and phase reversal switch.

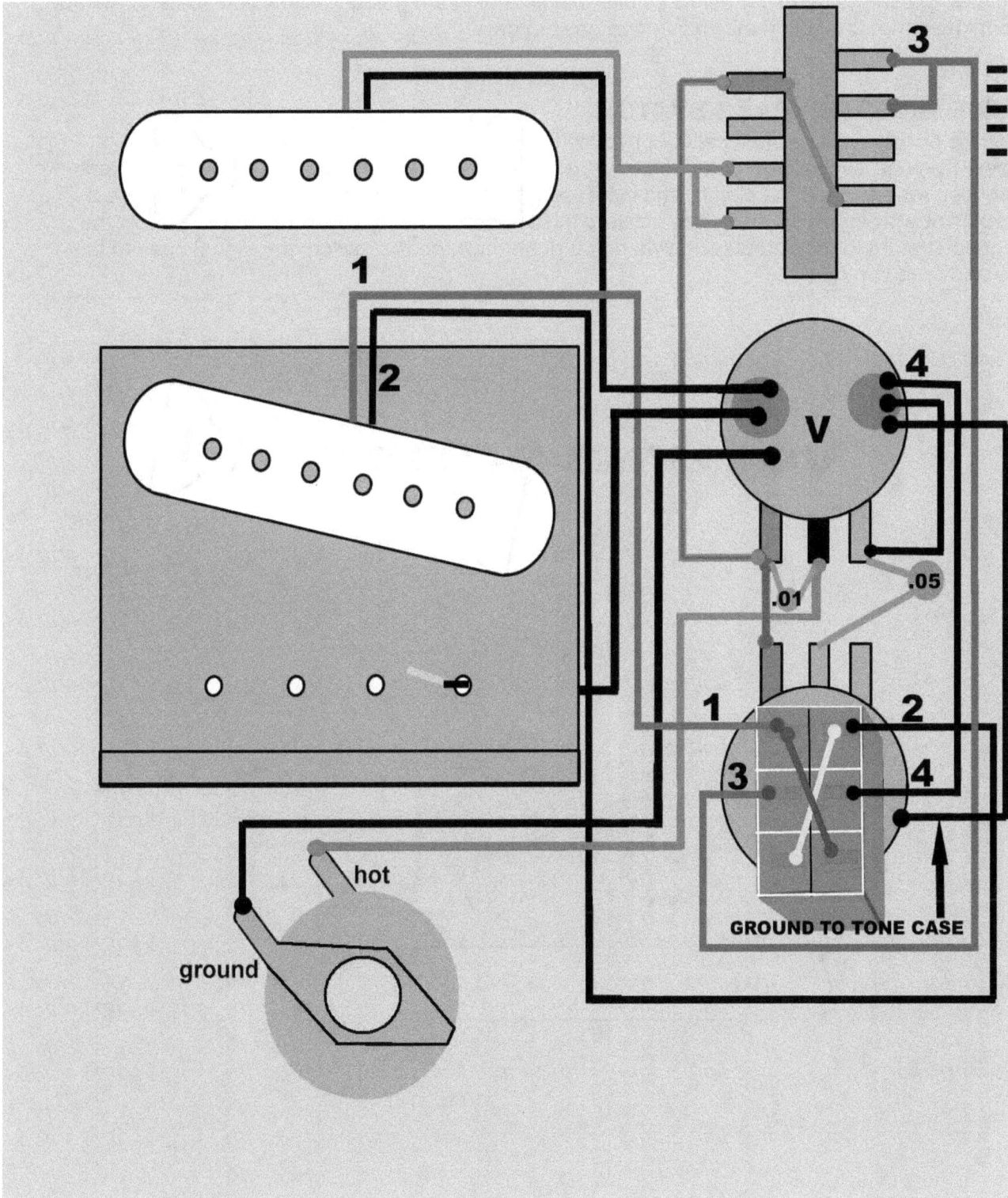

HOT ROD TECHNIQUES

The pros rarely play stock guitars like you or me. They usually incorporate some type of modification to their guitar to get out more useable sounds. I am going to show you some of the hot rod techniques that are both inexpensive and easy to do.

VOLUME BOOST/BYPASS SWITCH

The volume boost switch is often called a bypass switch, or treble boost switch. It works by bypassing the tone and volume potentiometers, and sending the signal straight to the output jack. This reduces resistance in the circuit, and increases the output of the high tones. You can use a **push pull pot** with an **on/on switch** to activate this bypass. When you pull up on the switch, the signal goes straight to the output jack. When you push down on the switch, the signal goes to the volume and tone controls.

VOLUME BOOST

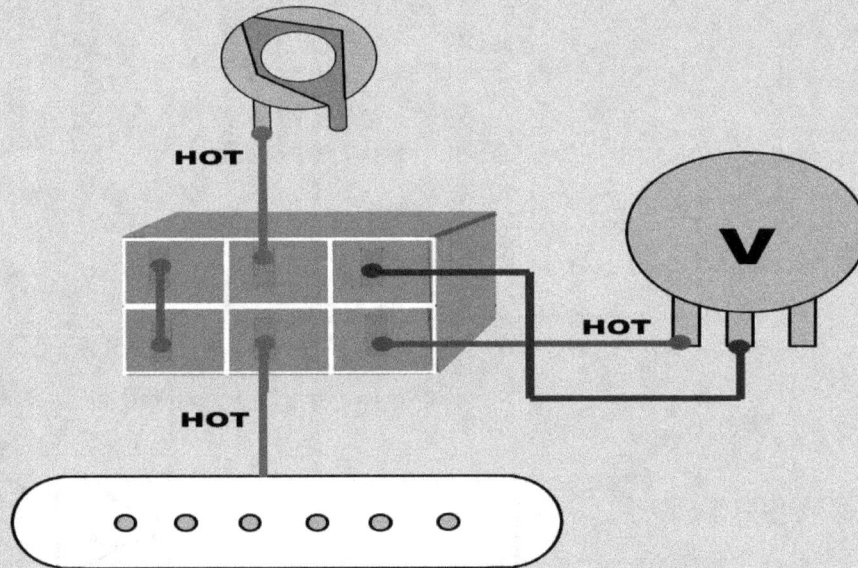

The example below shows the volume boost switch on a strat.

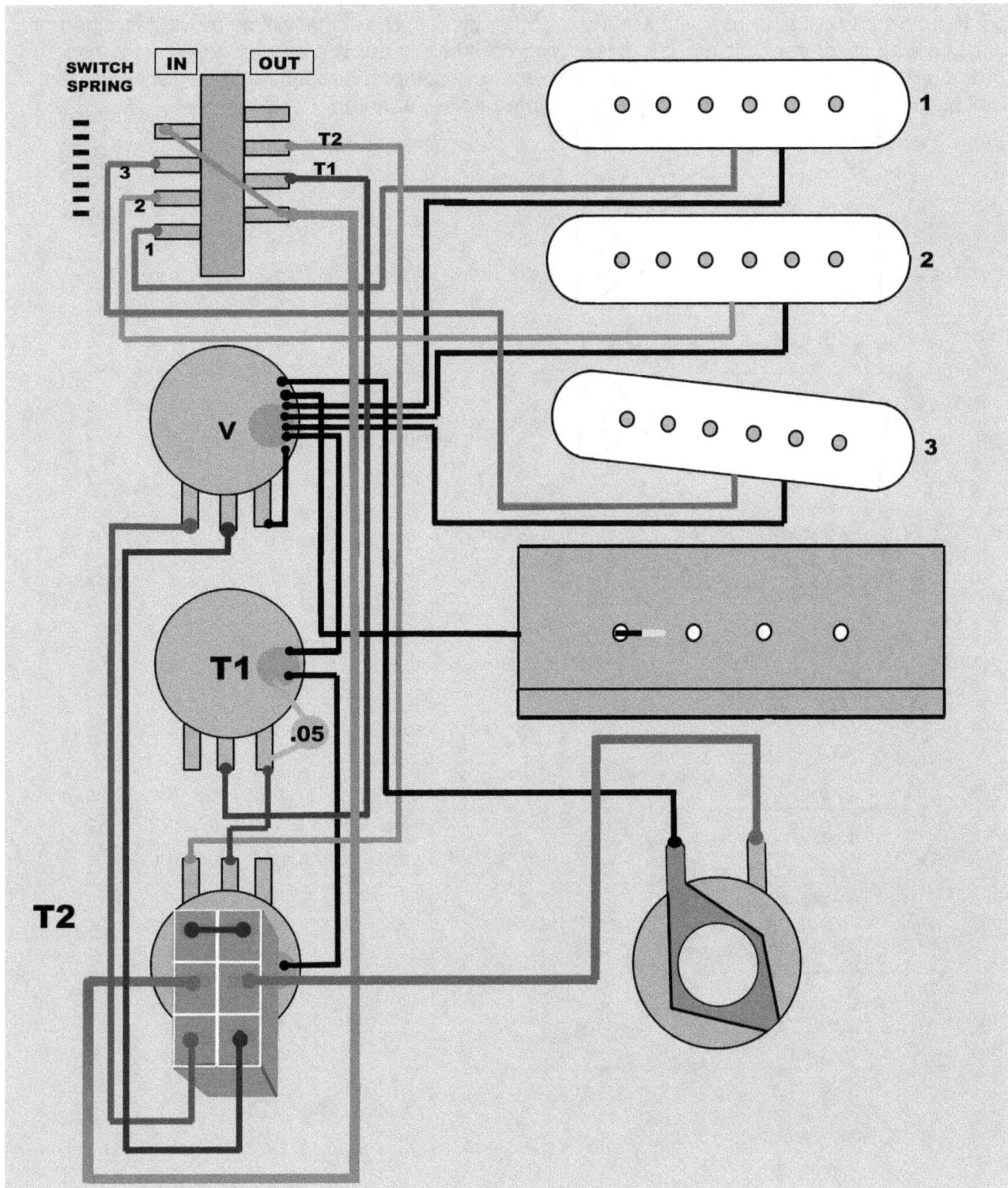

- 83 -

PHASE REVERSAL SWITCHES

Another way to utilize mini toggle switches involves phase switching. When you change the phase of a pickup, you are changing the direction of the electrical current flowing through the copper wires. Most pickups are wired to be in-phase with each other, and their signals usually move in the same direction. If a pickup is out of phase with itself, or another pickup, the signal will be moving in different directions in each coil, or each pickup. So at least two coils or pickups are needed to get a thinner, out of phase sound. The out of phase sound also has a lower output. Keep in mind that out of phase single coil pickups can sometimes produce an unwanted noise, or hum.

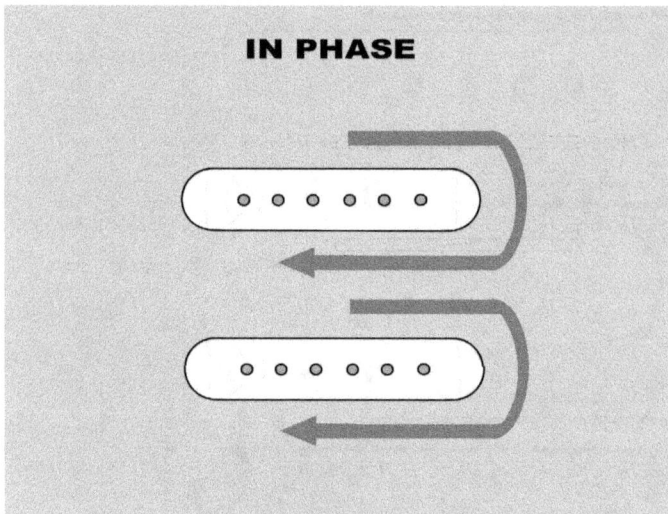

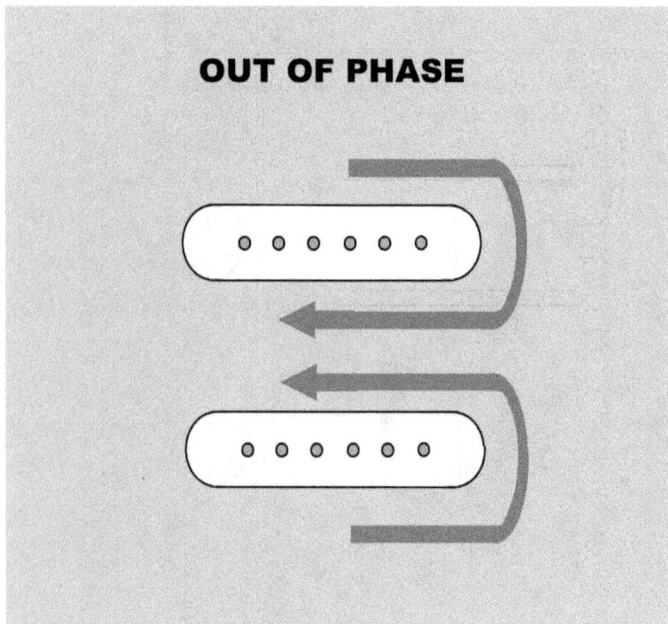

The next example shows how to change the phase of one pickup using a DPDT on-on switch. Just send the signal to the mini toggle before it enters the pickup selector switch, and also throw in some diagonal jumper wires. You only need to change the phase of one pickup to throw it out of phase with another pickup. It would be useless to change the phase of both pickups since it would just put them back in phase with each other.

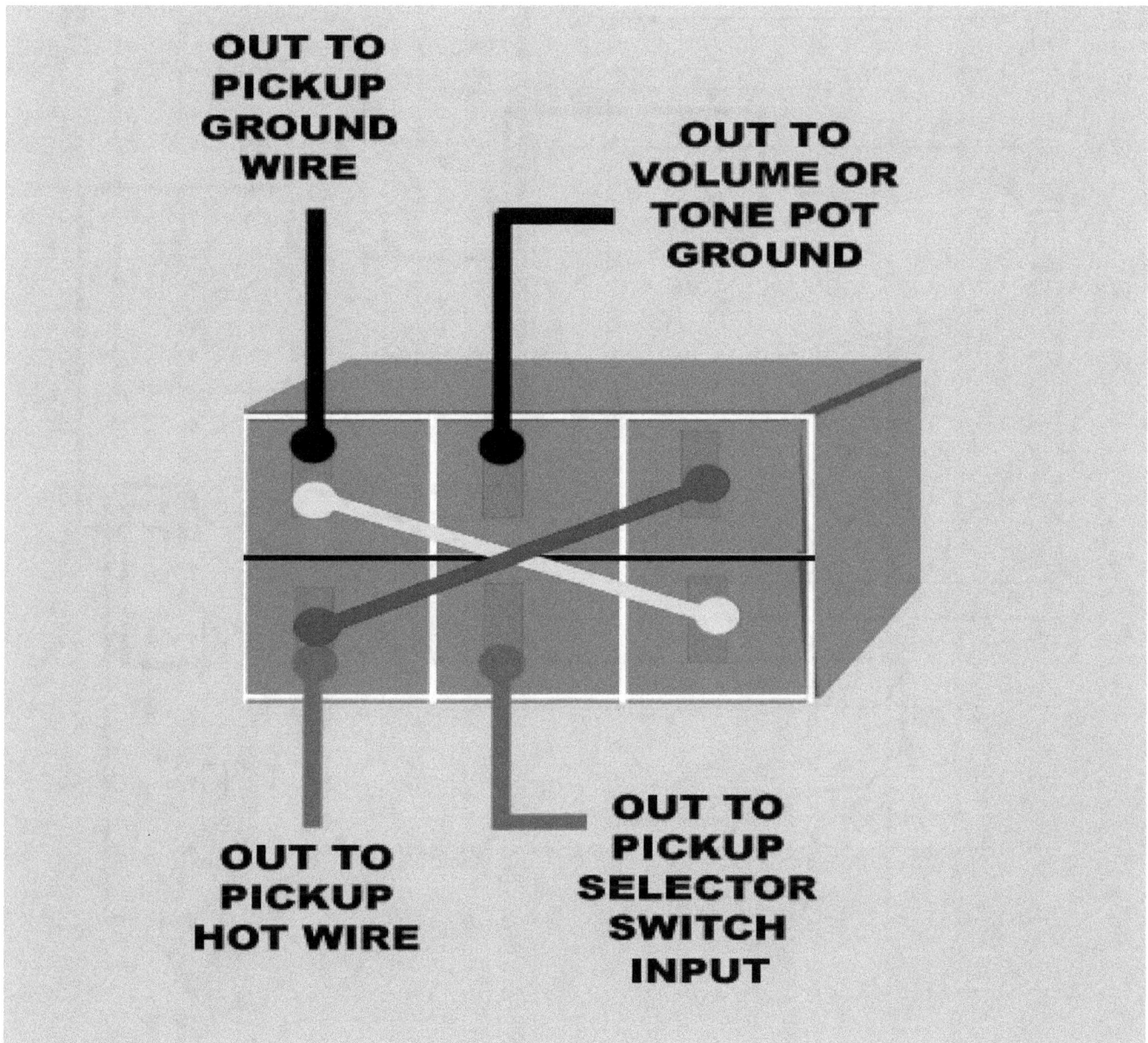

OUT TO PICKUP GROUND WIRE

OUT TO VOLUME OR TONE POT GROUND

OUT TO PICKUP HOT WIRE

OUT TO PICKUP SELECTOR SWITCH INPUT

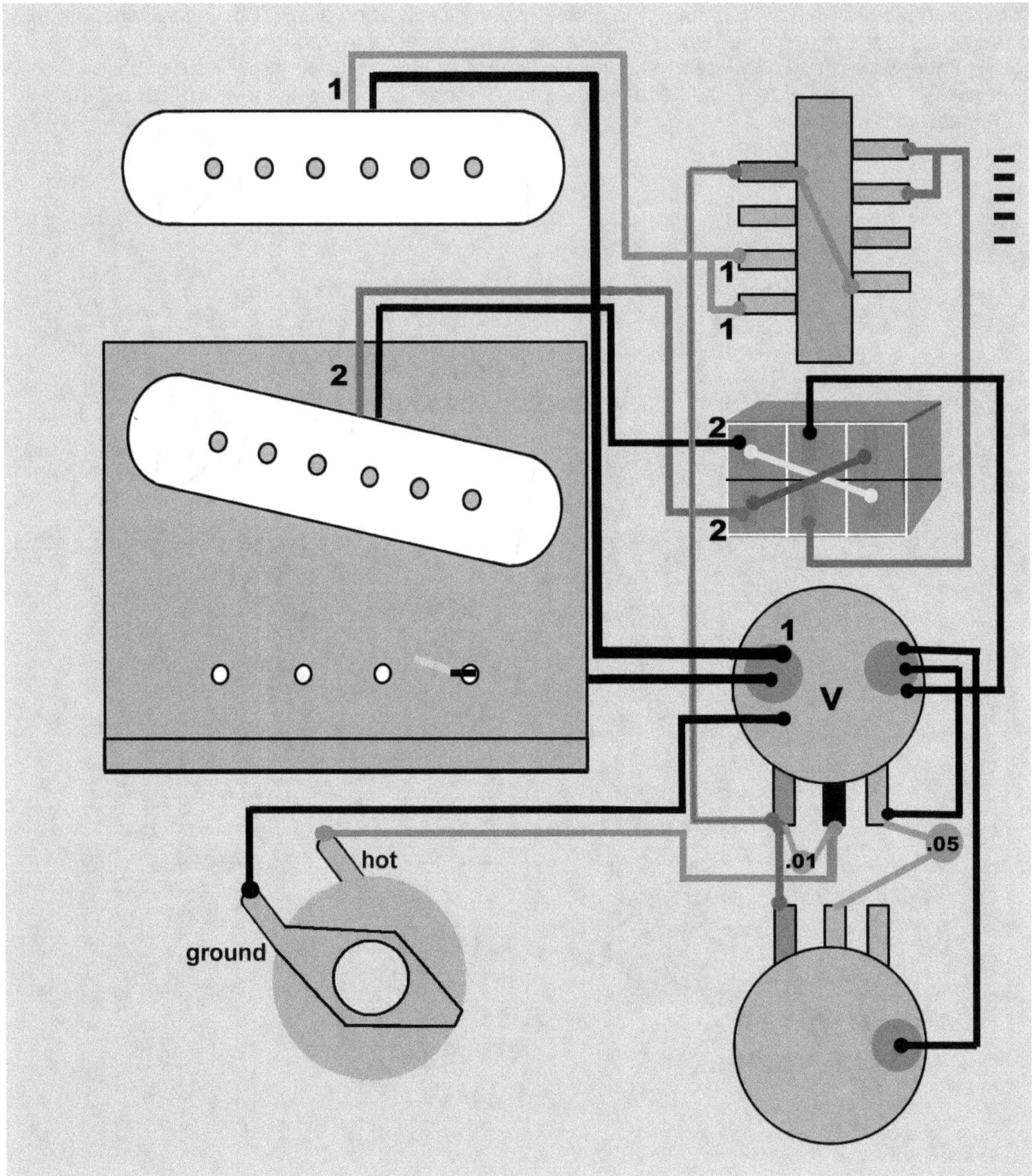

If you don't want to drill a hole for a mini toggle, you can use a push pull pot instead. It is a combination of a mini toggle switch and potentiometer.

Here is the same wiring with a push pull pot. For more info on push pull pots, check out the potentiometer section in this book.

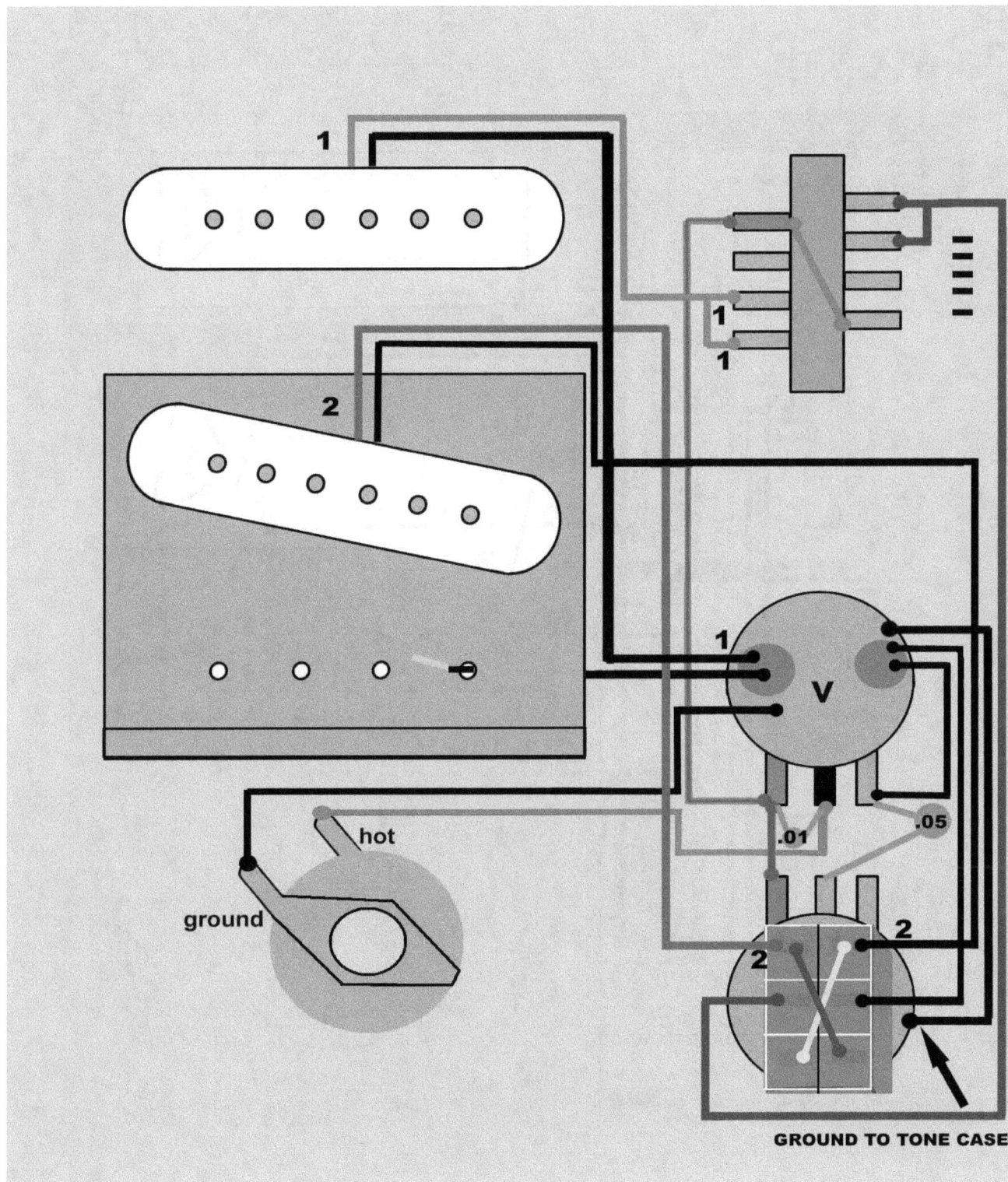

GROUND TO TONE CASE

If you want the middle pickup to go in or out of phase with the neck and bridge pickups in your strat, then you can wire the guitar like this.

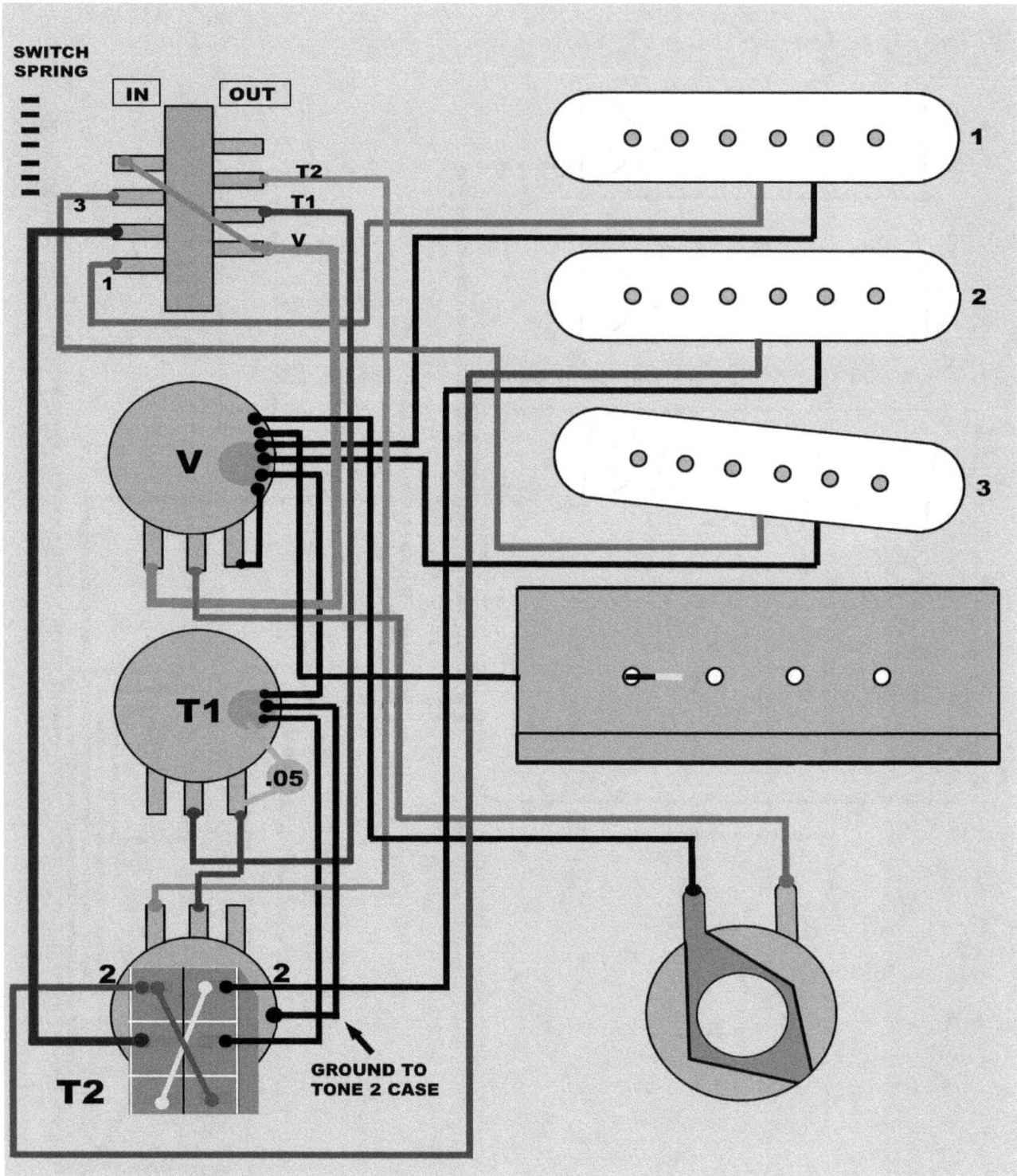

If you have a Les Paul, you can wire it this way to get the bridge pickup in or out of phase with the neck pickup. Notice how the 3-way switch sends the signal to the output jack. To make this wiring work, the push pull pot mini toggle switch sends the signal to the 3-way switch and volume pot, and then back to the push pull tone pot.

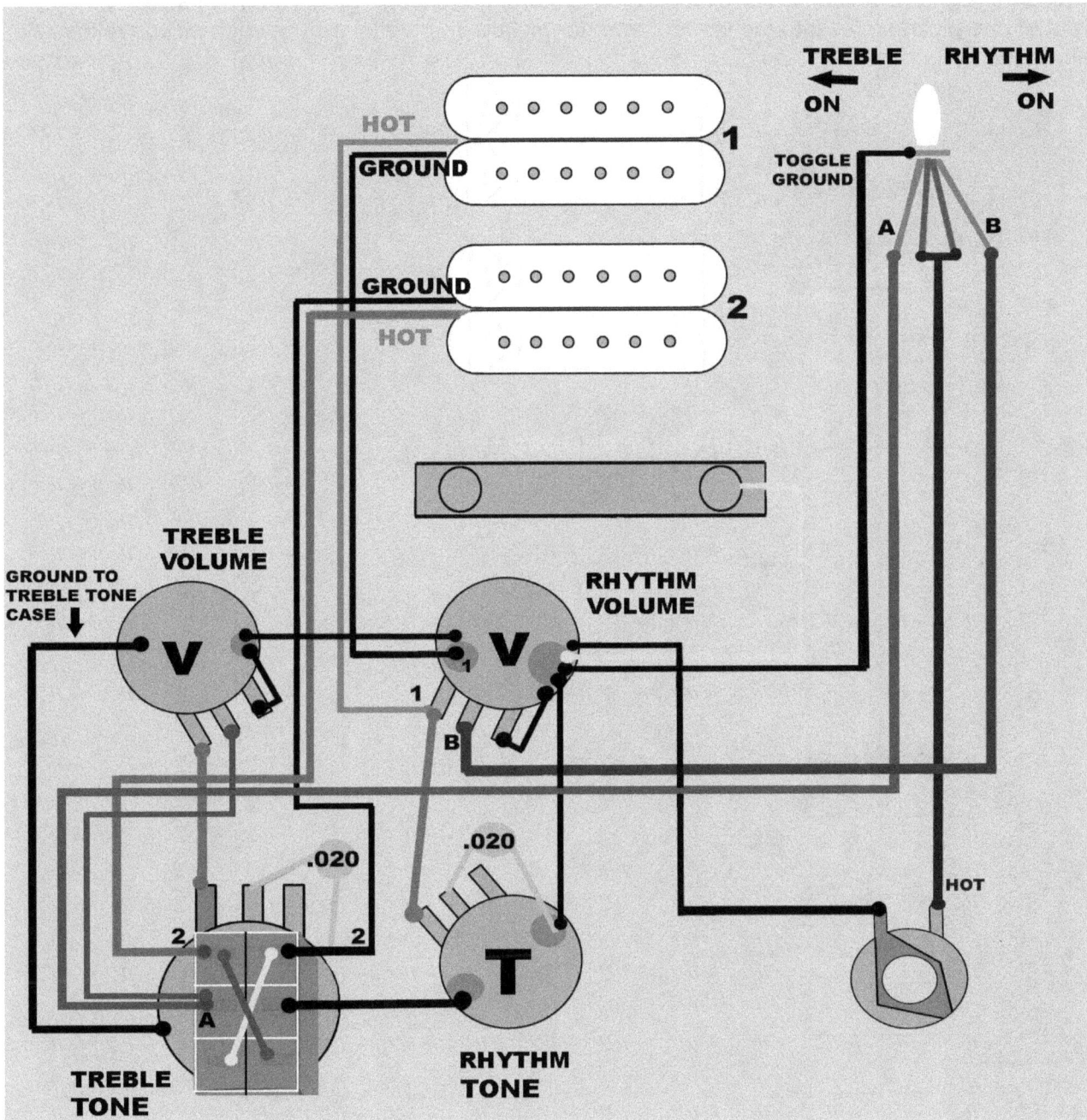

SERIES/PARALLEL WIRING

If you are looking to get more volume and midrange out of your pickups, you might want to try adding a series/parallel switch to your setup. Parallel wiring between two pickups is probably what you are used to by now. It's used in most guitars to add clarity to the sound. Series wiring is a little different. It produces a longer path with more resistance. This additional resistance prevents the higher tones from getting through the circuit, and allows more low/midrange tones to get through. In series wiring, the output of one pickup goes into the input of another pickup. In parallel wiring, each pickup takes its own path to the output.

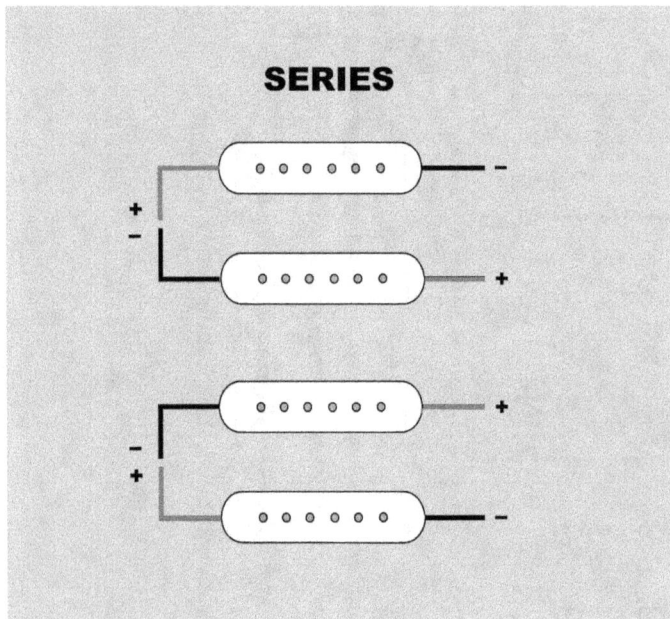

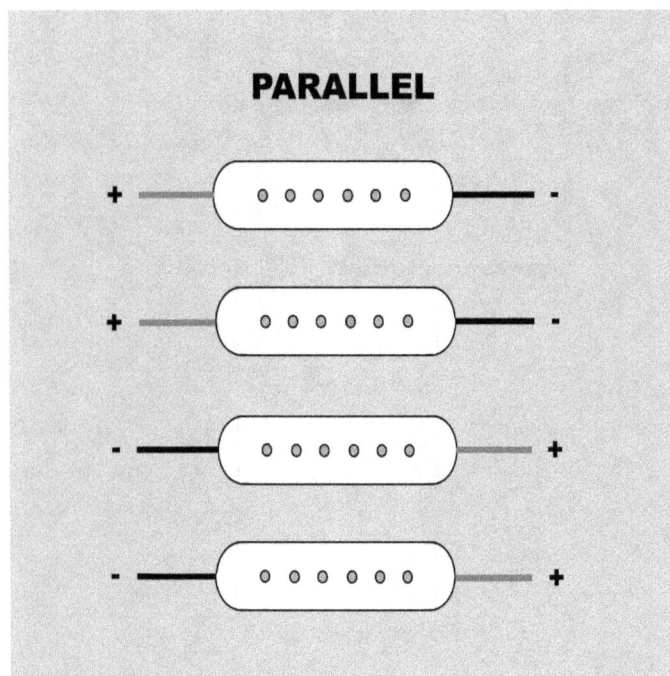

SERIES

PARALLEL

The diagram below shows how to wire a tele style guitar with a push pull pot that has a DPDT switch on it. When you have both pickups on at the same time, just pull up on the push pull pot, and the wiring will switch to series. The series wiring will be louder and have more lows than the parallel wiring. Notice the additional ground wire soldered to the neck pickup case. If you have a metal lipstick case covering your neck pickup, then you will need this ground wire to reduce unwanted noise when using the series selection.

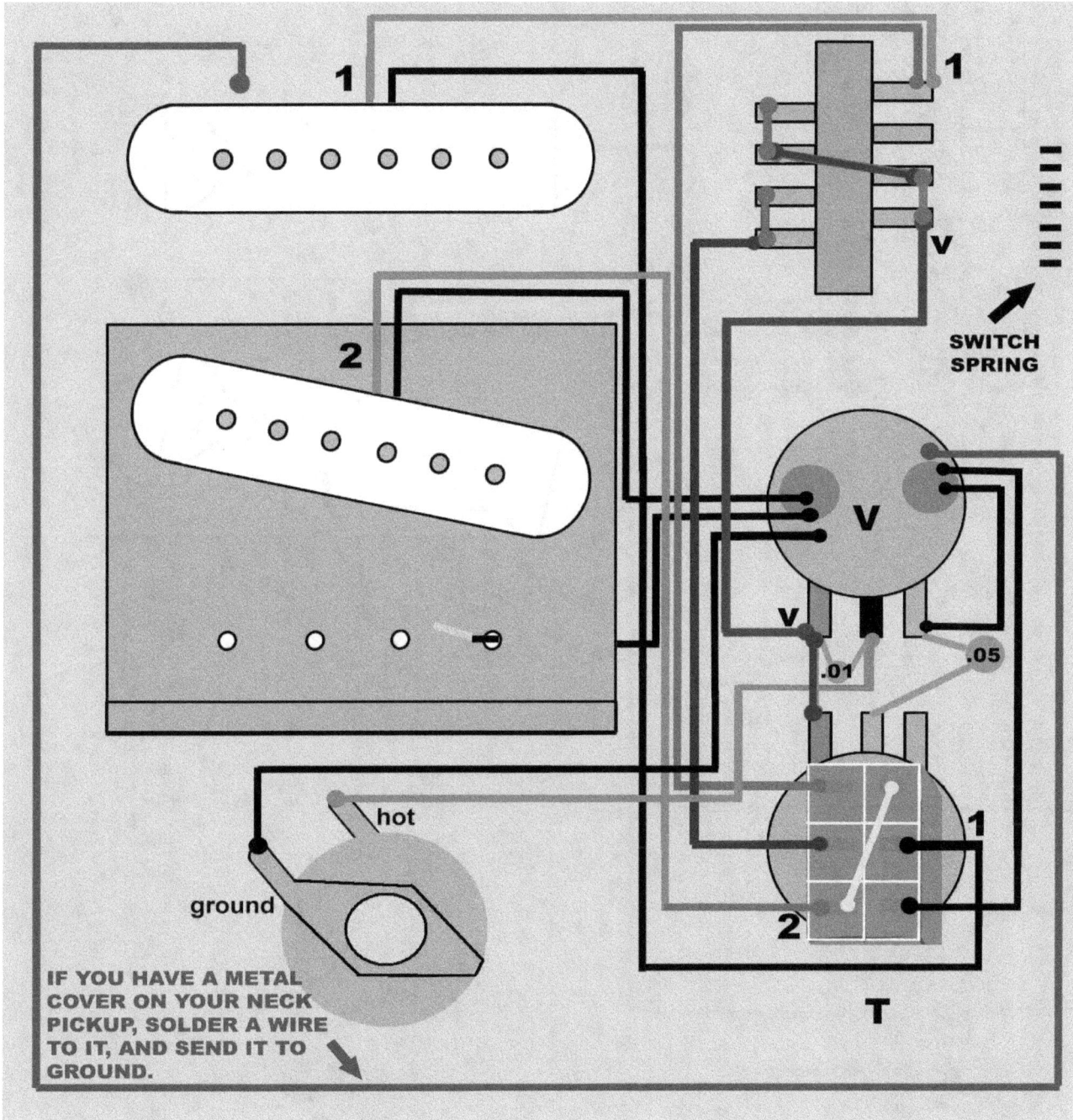

SWITCH
SPRING

hot

ground

IF YOU HAVE A METAL
COVER ON YOUR NECK
PICKUP, SOLDER A WIRE
TO IT, AND SEND IT TO
GROUND.

Now take a look at the strat style guitar with a series/parallel switch. It has 8 different sounds. When you pull out the push pull pot, you will have the neck and middle pickup in series in position 3, the bridge and middle pickup in parallel and in series with the neck pickup in position 4, and the bridge and neck pickup in series in position 5.

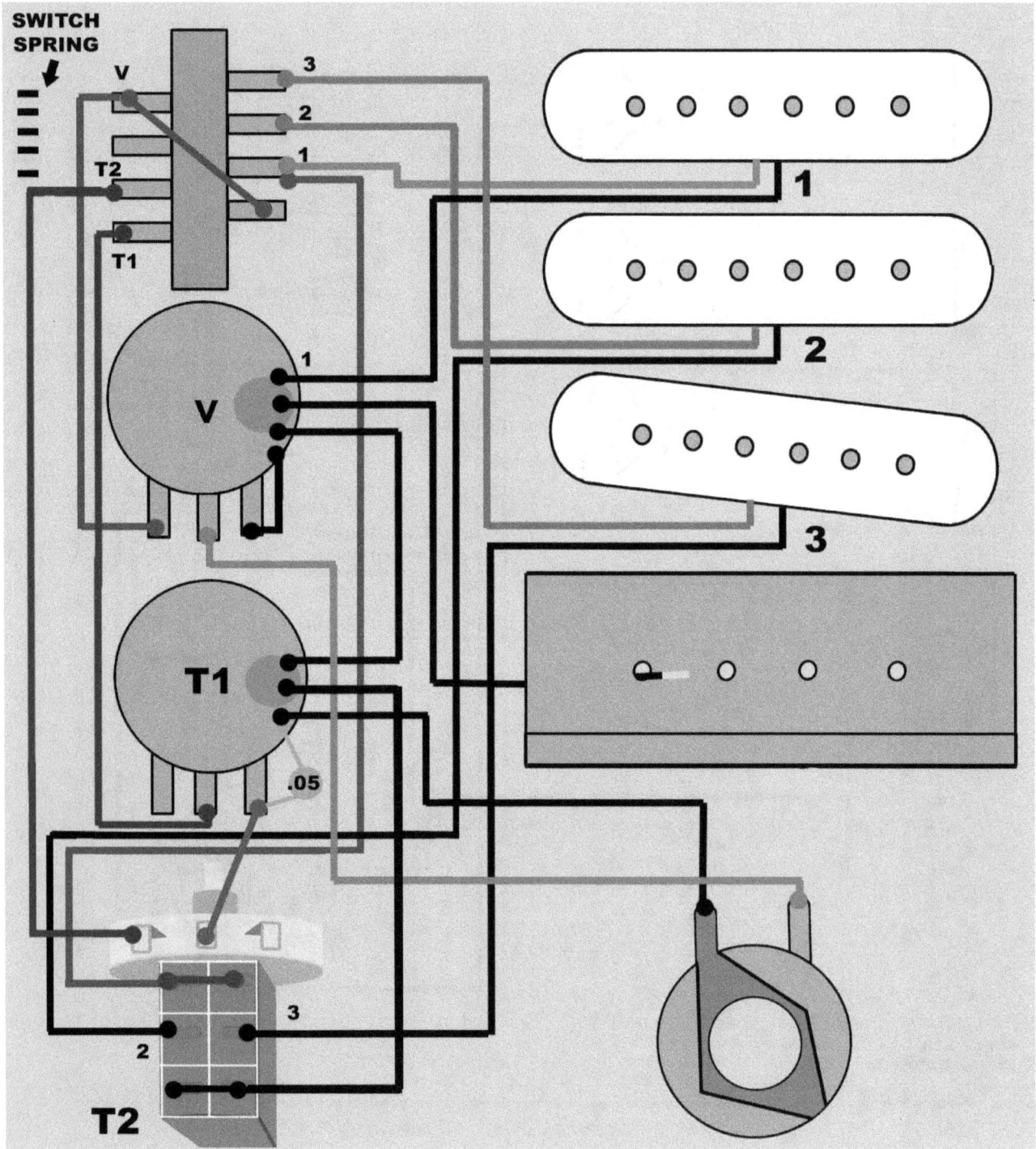

- 92 -

Finally, we have the Les Paul style guitar with the series/parallel wiring. When both pickups are on, just pull out the treble tone push pull pot, and it will switch both pickups to series.

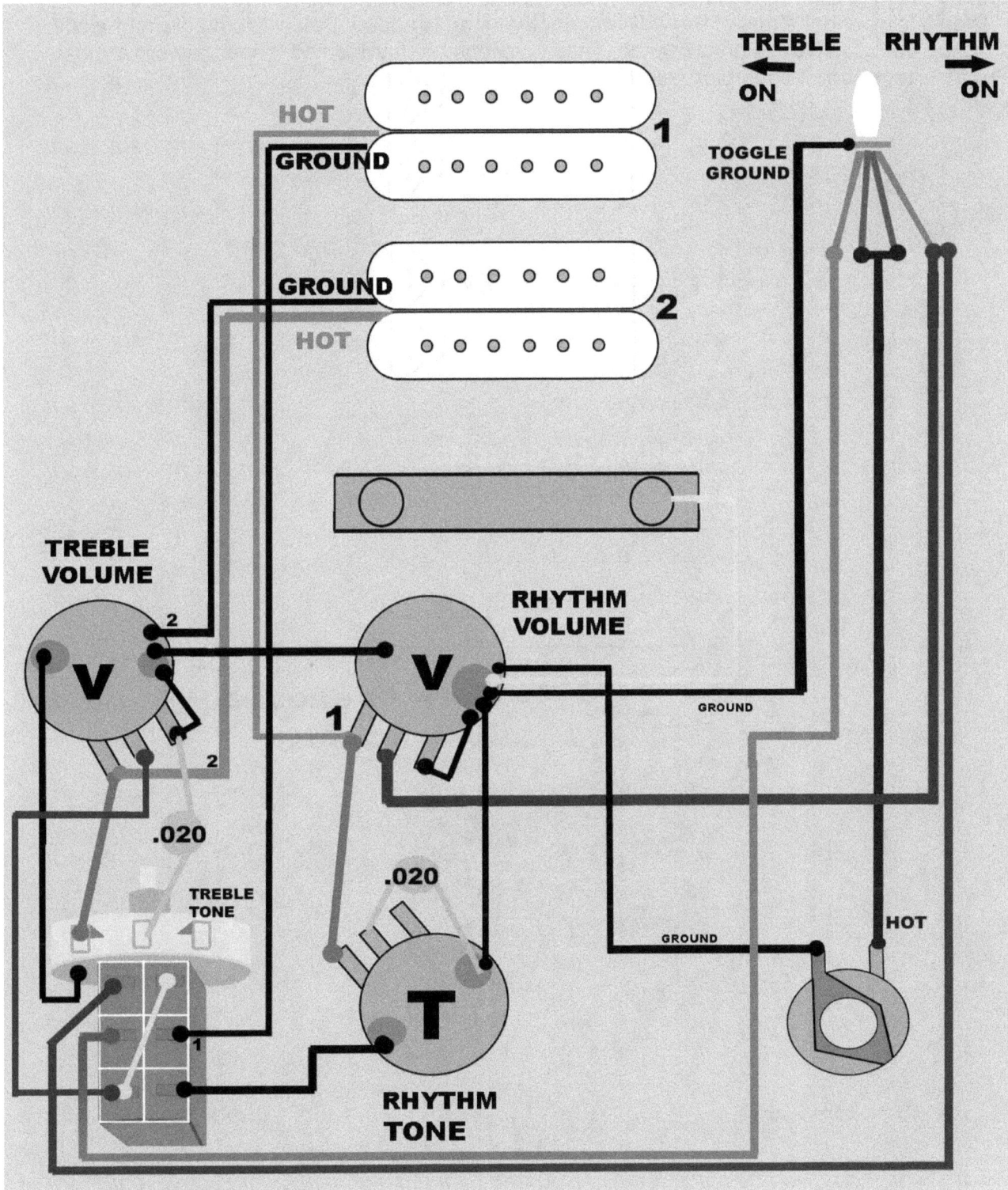

COIL TAP/COIL CUT

By far the most useful guitar hot rod technique is **coil cutting.** It gives you the benefits of both worlds. With a 4 wire pickup you can create a strat sound and a les paul sound at the flick of a switch. Note: coil cutting is often referred to as **coil tapping.** Coil tapping, however, involves single coil pickups that have 2 leads and a ground wire. Basically, the coil tapped pickup is wound halfway and a lead is added. Then it is wound the rest of the way and another lead is added. Below is a diagram of a coil tapped pickup hooked up to an on/on switch. These pickups are hard to find, especially since most sellers use the term "coil tapped pickups" to describe "coil cut pickups."

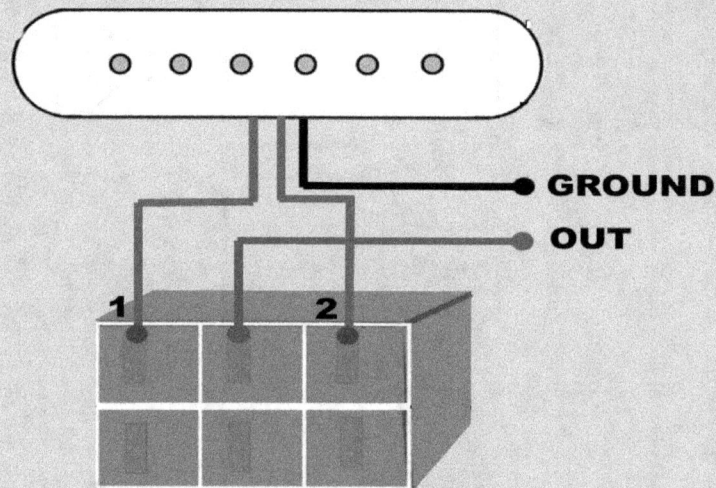

COIL TAP

Coil cutting is fairly easy to do with an **on/on/on switch** and a 4 wire humbucker. This setup will yield three different tones: north coil on, both coils on, and south coil on. Only two wires exit the on/on/on switch, a hot lead, and a ground lead. So it can be wired just like any 2 wire pickup once the signal leaves the switch.

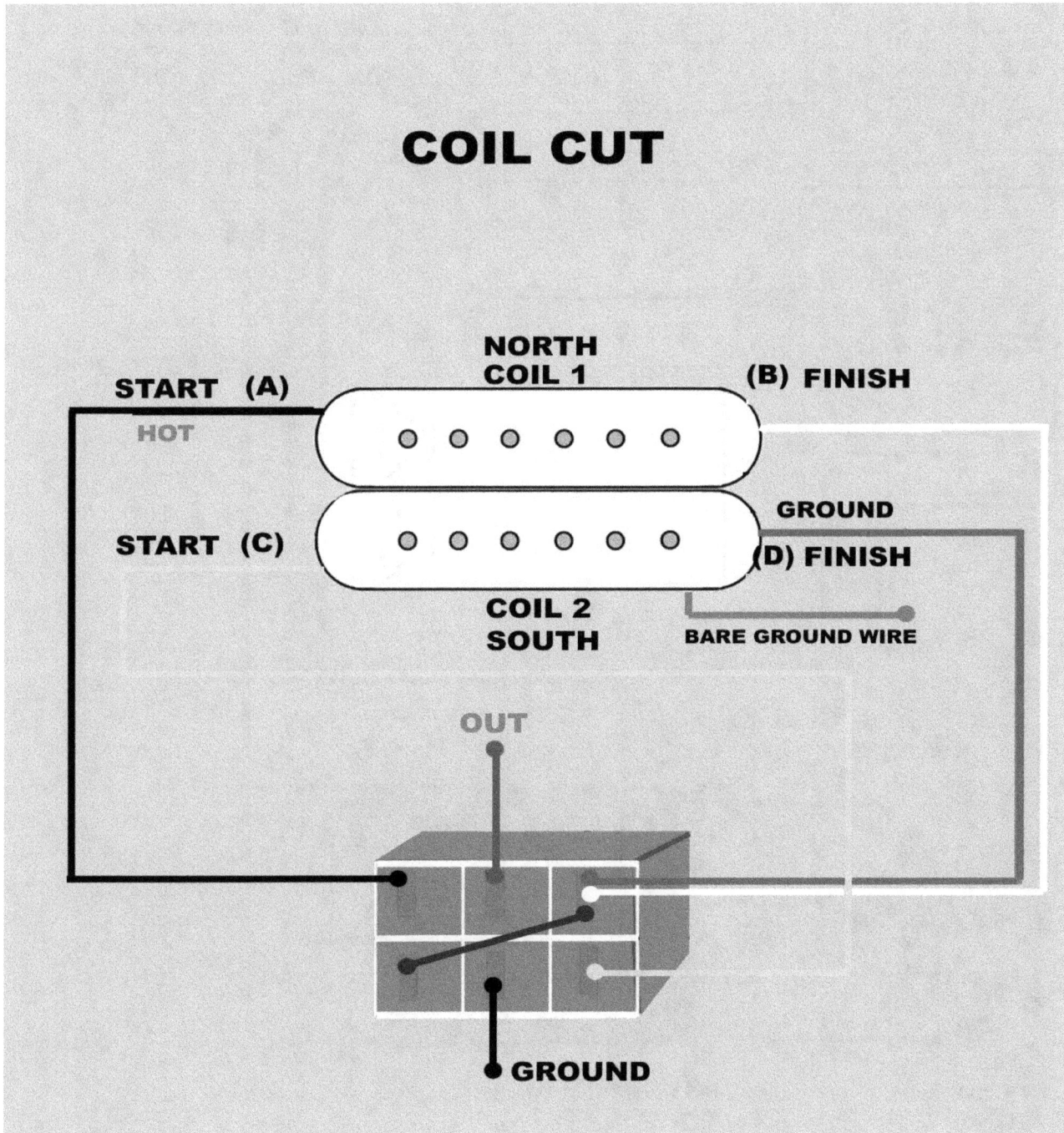

COIL CUT

START (A)   NORTH COIL 1   (B) FINISH

HOT

START (C)   GROUND   (D) FINISH

COIL 2 SOUTH   BARE GROUND WIRE

OUT

GROUND

Here is a Les Paul style guitar wired with two coil cut switches. See if you can figure how many tone options these 4 coils have.

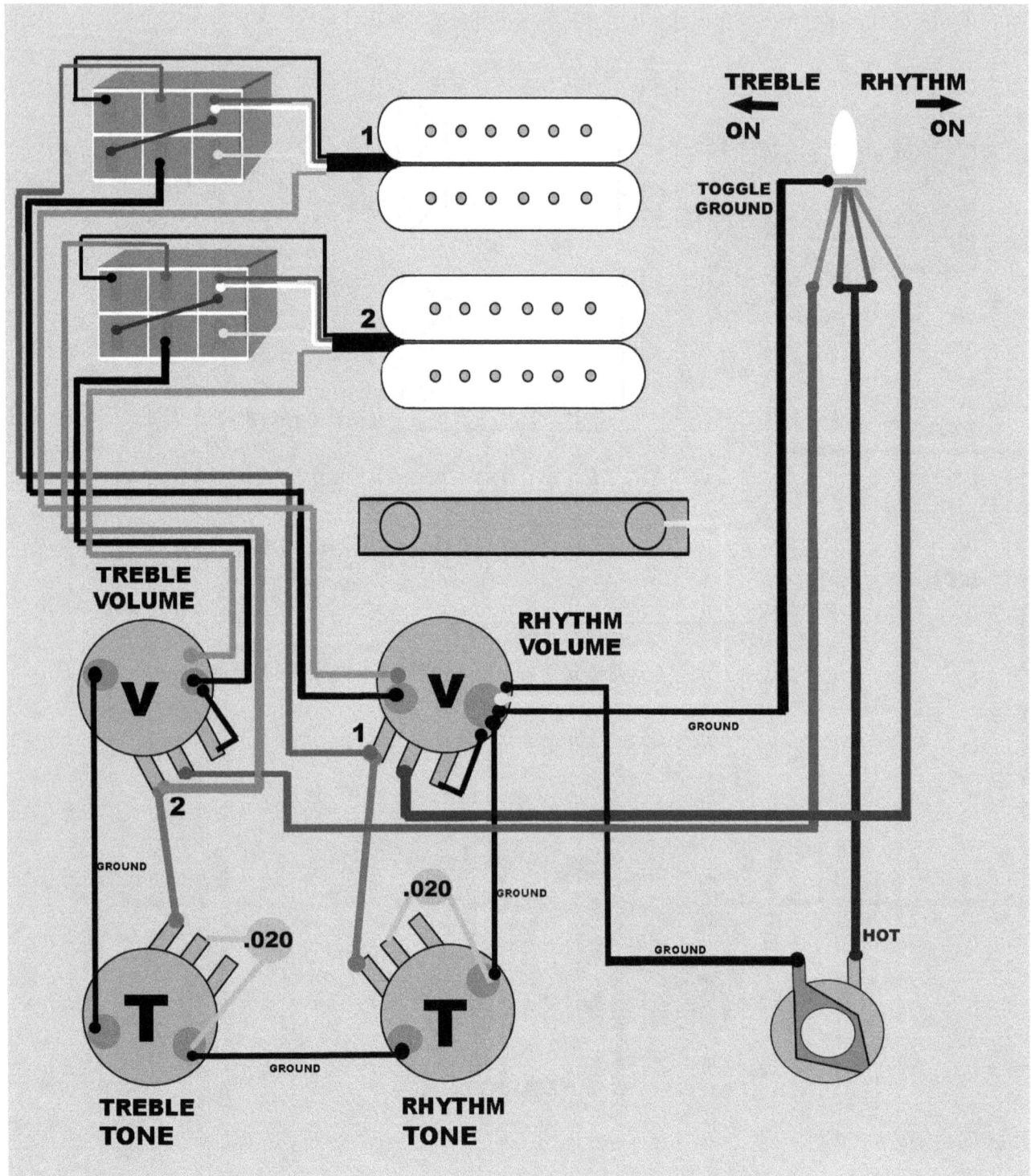

TREBLE ← ON   RHYTHM → ON

TOGGLE GROUND

1

2

TREBLE VOLUME
V

RHYTHM VOLUME
V

1

2

GROUND

GROUND

GROUND

.020

.020

GROUND

GROUND

HOT

TREBLE TONE
T

RHYTHM TONE
T

GROUND

- 96 -

QUESTIONS AND ANSWERS

Question: Which lug on the output jack is hot, and which lug is a ground?
 There are two lugs on the jack. One of them is attached to the prong. That one is hot. Sometimes the hot lug has a different shape, and is notched.

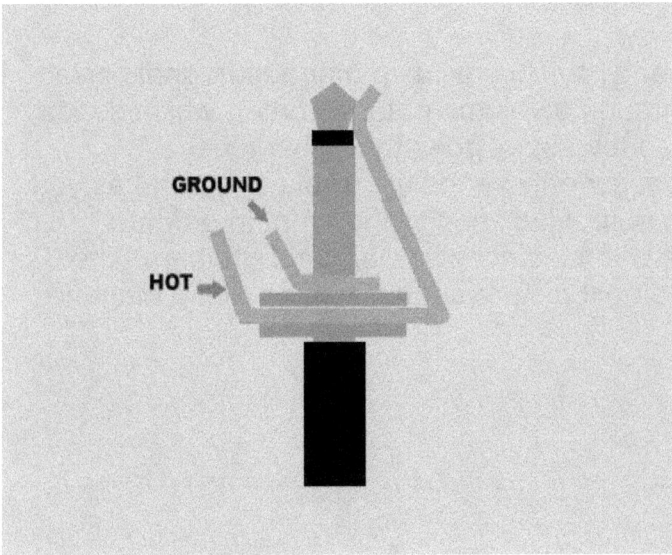

If you are using active pickups or a preamp inside your guitar, then you will probably need to use a stereo output jack. It has one addition lug that receives the signal from a 9 volt battery.

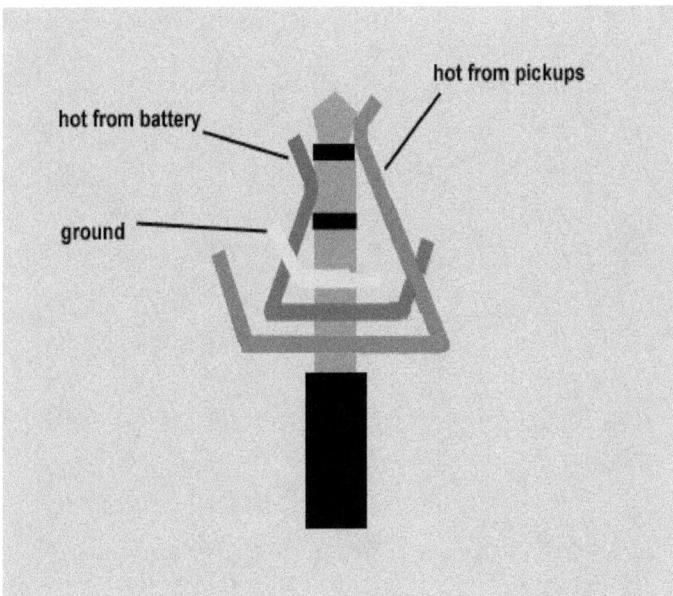

Question: What do the colors on the wires mean?

You have probably noticed by now that most hot wires are colored, like white, red, or yellow, and most ground wires are black. Although most pickup companies do not use the same color codes, most ground wires will be black. You should check with the manufacturer to see what color code your pickups have just to be on the safe side.

Question: How do pickups work?

Basically, pickups are magnets wrapped in copper wire. They pick up magnetic signals given off by vibrating strings. The signal gets carried through a volume potentiometer, which sends the signal to ground to decrease the volume. Then the signal goes through a tone potentiometer connected to a capacitor. The capacitor only sends the treble to ground as you turn the tone control. Then the signal goes to the output jack and to the amp. In order to complete the circuit, you need to ground all parts with electricity flowing through them. The 3 way switch turns different pickups off and on. The next picture shows a basic wiring diagram with one pickup and one volume control.

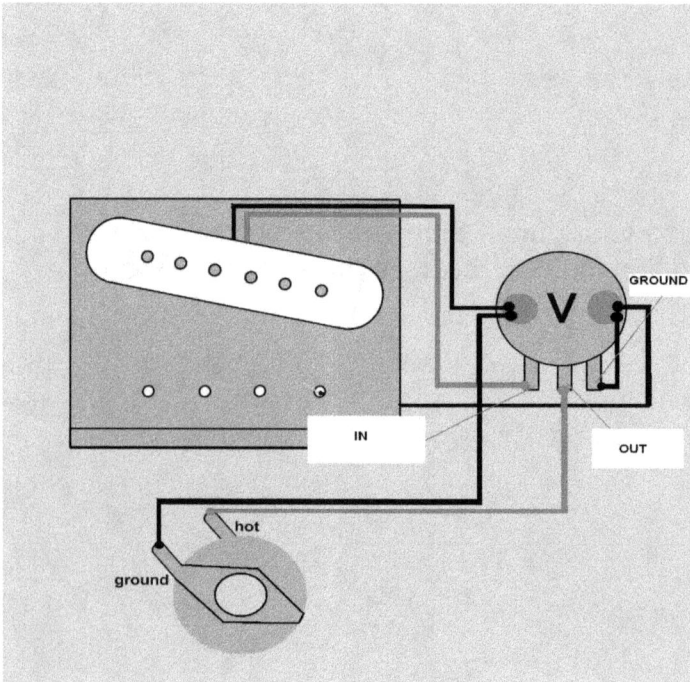

Question: Why do some pickups have staggered pole pieces?
Staggering the magnet poles increases or decreases the magnetic output of each string. So have a higher output should have lower magnets to give the guitar a balanced volume on all example, my strat has a higher output on the B and E strings, so to compensate for that, the poles on the B and E strings.

Question: Which pickups have more unwanted noise, single coil, or double coil?
This problem, called 60 cycle hum, is common among single coil pickups. It occurs when the pickup basically picks up interference from an alternating current electrical supply that is nearby. Proper grounding and proper wire shielding can reduce this unwanted noise. Double coil pickups have less noise, but also have less treble. Many guitarists prefer single coils for their vintage guitar sound.

Question: Do you have any soldering tips?
Before you get started with the pickup wiring, you will need to add solder to the ends of all lugs and wires. This will make the soldering job go much quicker. If you take too long to solder a connection, you can damage a potentiometer, or capacitor. After you solder a wire to a lug, do not move it for at least 3 seconds. Any movement can cause a cold, or bad joint.

Question: What is a good way to prevent electrical shock?
Often, getting shocked while playing guitar is the result of faulty wiring, not necessarily in your guitar, but in the outlets that your equipment is plugged into. Faulty wiring has been a problem at some clubs. It all depends on who does the wiring, and if they know what they are doing. One way to protect yourself is to get an AEMC Outlet Tester. It can detect faulty wiring in three-wire receptacles, open grounds & neutrals, and reversed hot/ground connections. You can get one at Amazon.com. You can also get a wireless system for your guitar to increase your protection.

Question: What is the cheapest way to change the sound of my guitar?
Change the pickup height. The closer the pickups are to the strings, the stronger the signal. The farther away they are, the weaker the signal. If your pickups are too close to the strings, they can sound too thick and distorted. Or you can just change the strings on your guitar. The thicker the strings will give you a warmer sound. Or change the potentiometers. Higher value pots like a 500K or 1 Meg will give you a brighter sound. Most strats use 250K pots. Last but not least, change the capacitor on your tone control. A stronger capacitor will give you a muddier sound with more bass.

Question: What effect do magnets have on a pickup?
Basically, the stronger the magnet, the stronger the pull is on the strings. The stronger magnetic field will slow down the string vibrations and give your pickups a warmer sound. Weaker magnets will pull less and give you a brighter sound. To test this out, raise your neck pickup so it almost touches the strings. Notice how the sound is muddier than usual.

Question: What is impedance?
Impedance is the resistance in a circuit. In other words, the more resistance you have in a circuit, the weaker the signal will be. If you wanted pickups that are as strong as humanly possible, then you would need to eliminate all sources of impedance, like potentiometers and capacitors. Impedance also affects the tone of a guitar pickup. Adding more resistance in a circuit will cause a boost in midrage and bass levels.

Question: What is an active pickup?
It is a pickup that has its own preamp to boost the gain and volume, while reducing unwanted noise. Emg 85 pickups, which are played by the heavy metal band Metallica, are a good example of some popular active pickups. Active pickups also have their own power source, like a 9 volt battery.

Question: What type of wire is used in guitar electronics?
Most guitars use a 22 AWG wire with a braided or teflon shield.

Question: Why does a telecaster have such a bright, twangy sound?
The telecaster uses a copper plated steel bridge which helps to increase the strength of the bridge pickup's magnetic field. This gives it a brighter, twangy sound.

Question: How do you wire a Fender Esquire that has only one pickup?
On the next page is a basic single pickup wiring diagram for telecasters using one pickup. this with either the bridge or neck pickup. The pickup will have a volume and tone control. plenty of good sounds out of this setup. If you want to play around with the tone, you can ι or weaker capacitor. Adding a stronger capacitor sends more treble to the ground, and giv bass tones. Note: there are many ways to wire pickups to the pots. This is just one examp

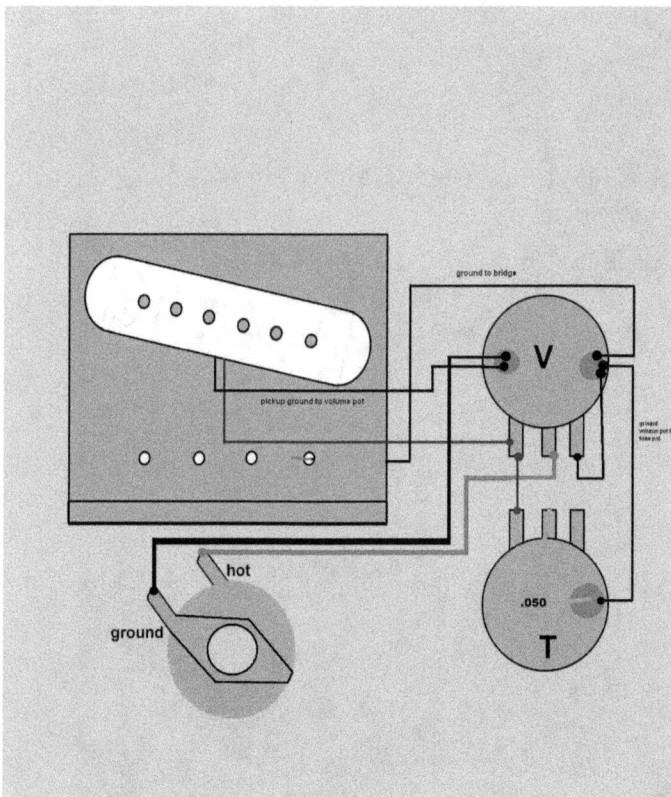

Question: How do you use a multimeter?
Multimeters can be used to check the resistance of pickups, potentiometers, leads, and speakers. If you need to know how "hot" a pickup is, then just connect each multimeter

lead to the hot and ground pickup wire and take a reading. Make sure the multimeter is set to the 20K Ohms setting. The tele neck pickup shown below came in at around 5.76K Ohms. If you don't get a reading, then the pickup needs repair.

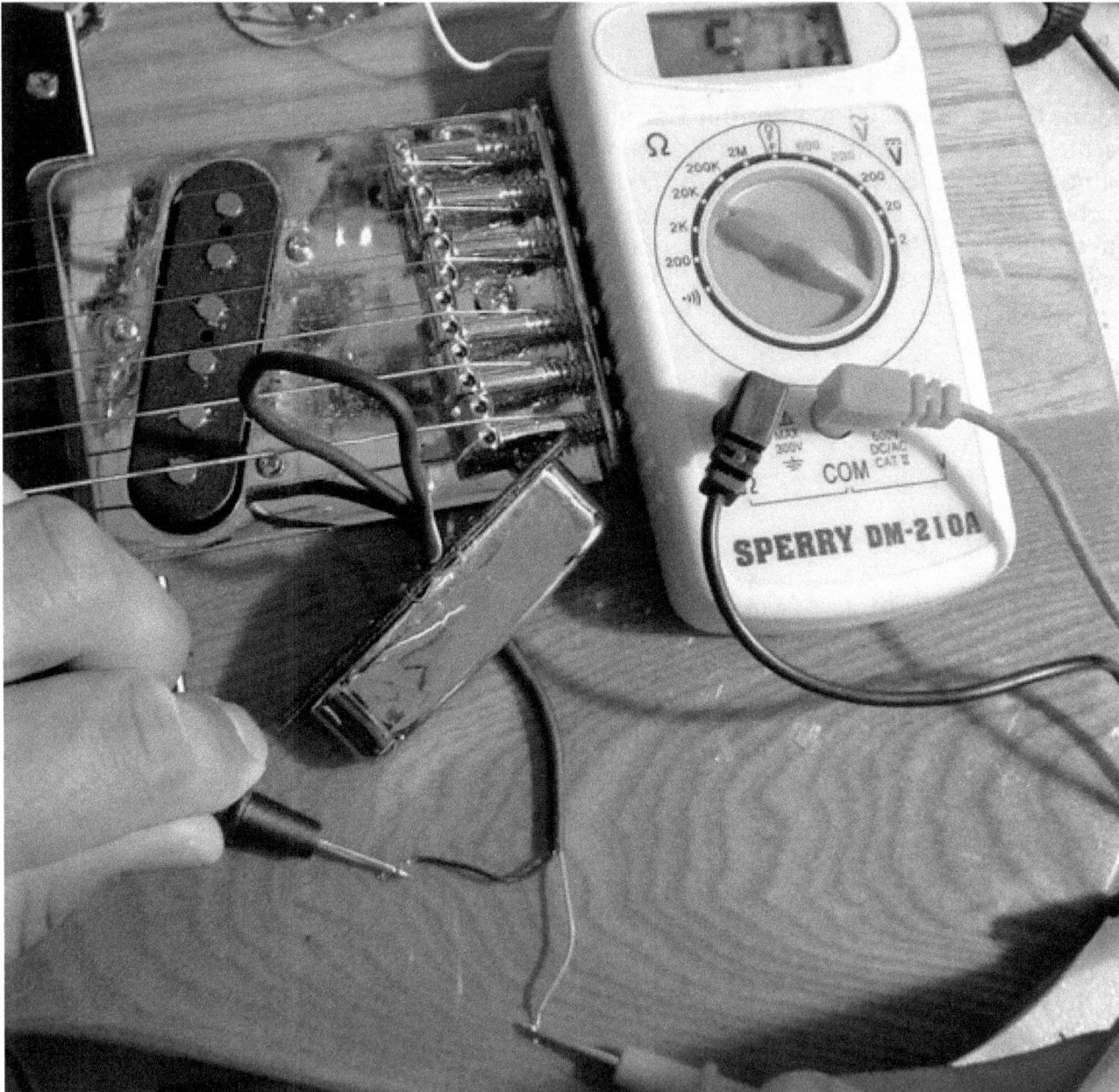

Is your tone or volume pot working? Check it out by placing a multimeter lead on the two end lugs. If you have a 250K pot, then you can expect a reading around 230K - 260K.

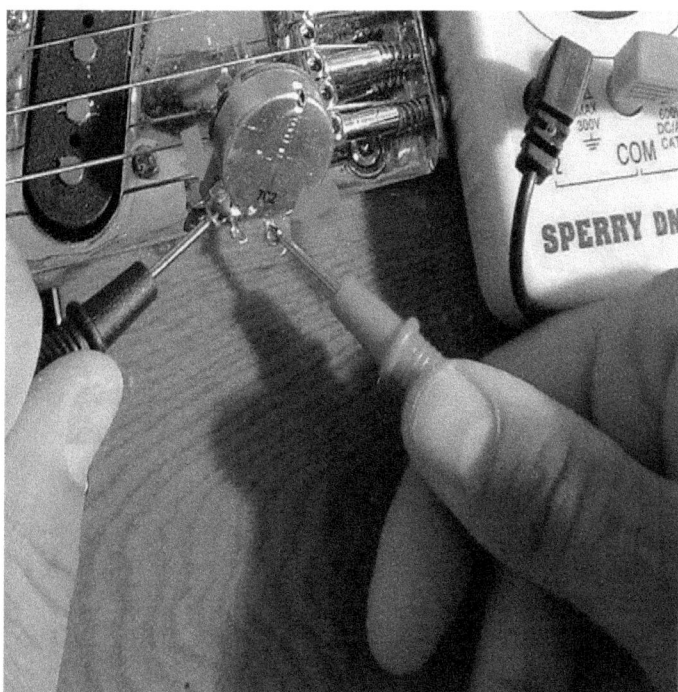

Question: How do you figure out the color codes on a 4 wire pickup?
You can use a multimeter to figure out which pickup wires belong to which coil. Switch the multimeter to the 20K Ohms setting. This will give you a reading up to 20,000 Ohms. Pick out one of the 4 shielded pickup wires, and then touch it to one of the multimeter leads. Now touch the other multimeter lead to every other remaining wire. Out of those remaining wires, only one wire will give a reading on the multimeter. The two wires that give a reading belong to the same coil. The two wires that are left will also give a reading, and will belong to the other coil. The 5th bare wire always goes to ground.

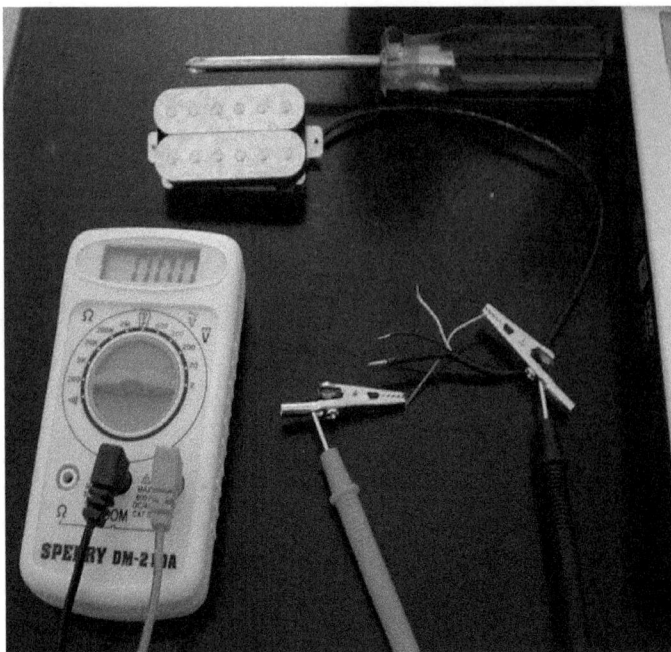

Now Set your multimeter to the 2 Volts setting. Attach some alligator clips to your two leads from the multimeter, and then connect them to two of the wires from the same coil. In the case below, I connected the green and red wires. Take a screwdriver and tap the poles on one of the pickup coils. Now remove the screwdriver. Notice how the reading on the multimeter goes positive, and then negative, or negative and then positive, and then back to zero? We are looking for the multimeter to give a positive reading when the screwdriver touches the poles, and a negative reading when it gets pulled away from the poles. If you are getting a negative first reading, switch the leads on the multimeter around. In this case, I had to remove the red multimeter lead from the red pickup wire, and attach it to the green pickup wire. I then connected the black multimeter lead to the red pickup wire. Now when the screwdriver taps the coil, it gives a positive reading first, and then a negative reading.

Next, let's figure out which coil these wires go to. Do the screwdriver test on the top coil, and then on the bottom coil. You will notice that one coil always gives a stronger reading than the other coil. In this case, it is the top coil. It gets a reading up to .099 before going negative. The bottom coil only goes up to .014, so we now know that the red and green wires belong to the top coil. The green wire will be called the start and the red wire will be the finish (the green wire is attached to the red multimeter lead). Next, you need to determine if the coil has a north or south polarity. This can easily be done with a magnet polarity tester from stewmac.com. They cost around $6. Just touch it to each pickup coil to determine the polarity. In this case, the top coil's polarity is south.

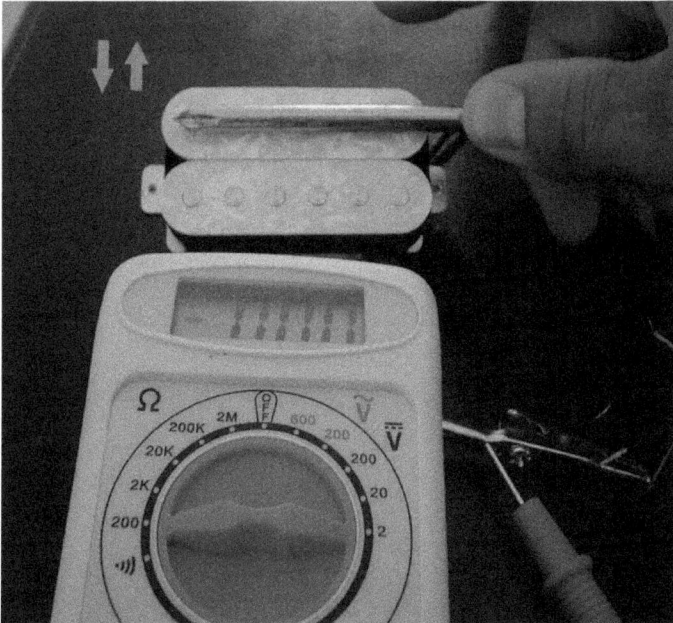

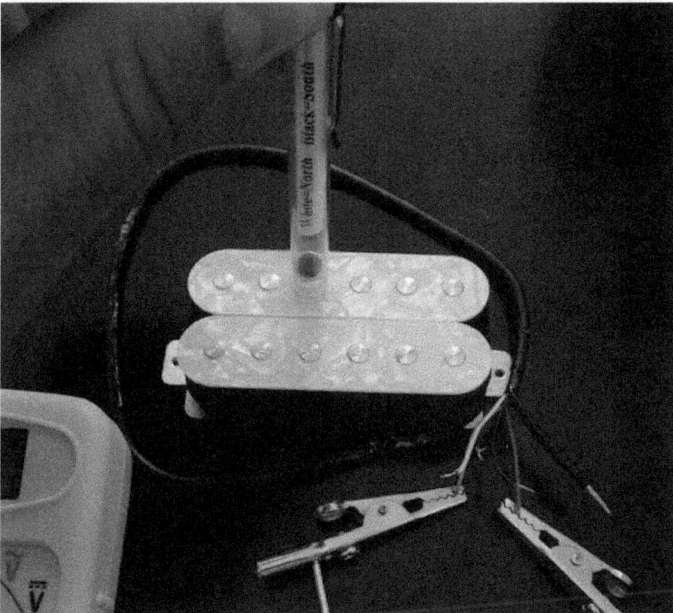

Let's move on to the next set of wires. I get a positive first reading when I connect the red multimeter lead to the black pickup wire, and the black multimeter lead to the white pickup wire. So the black wire will be the start, and the white wire will be the finish. The bottom coil also gives a stronger reading (up to .135) than the top coil (up to .016), so these wires belong to the bottom coil. Now check the polarity. The polarity tester shows a north polarity. Coil one and two are now done.

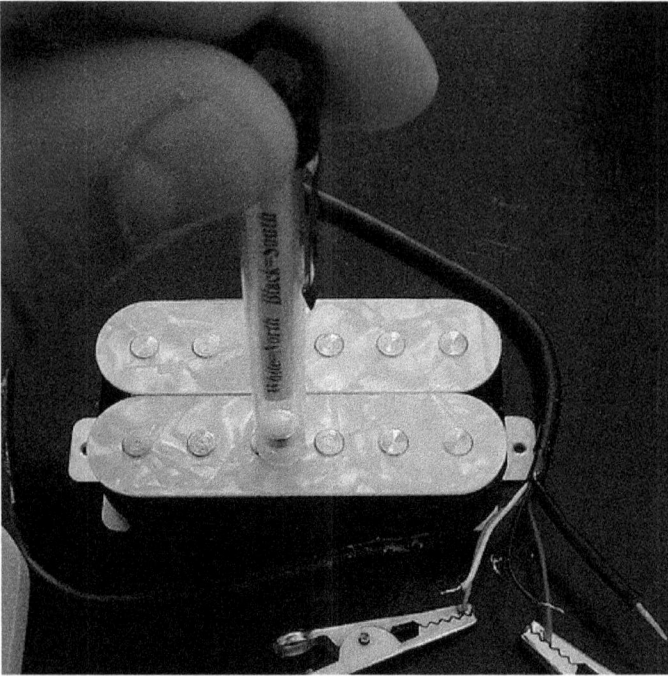

Here is the wiring diagram for this pickup. This pickup uses the same color codes as Seymour Duncan pickups.

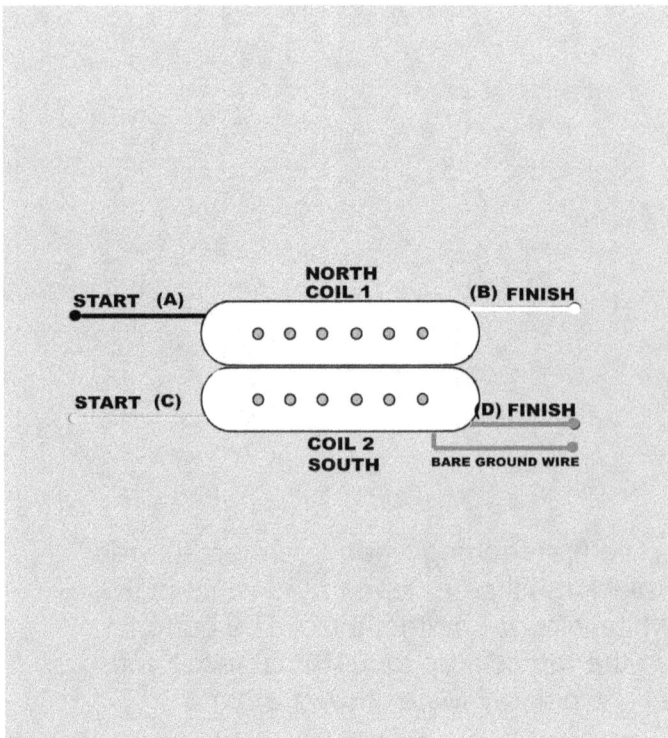

START (A) NORTH COIL 1 (B) FINISH

START (C) COIL 2 SOUTH (D) FINISH BARE GROUND WIRE

Question: What are some wiring options for a humbucking pickup?

I'm going to use the pickup I just described as an example. The first diagram below shows the series out of phase wiring, which is typical for most humbuckers. Being out of phase cancels the hum, and the series link adds a low/midrange boost. There is quite a bit of confusion out there regarding in and out of phase pickups. Although the electric current is actually in phase, the sound signal is out of phase. With that being said, if you visit 100 websites on series/parallel wiring, 50 of them will say humbuckers are wired in phase, and 50 will say they are wired out of phase.

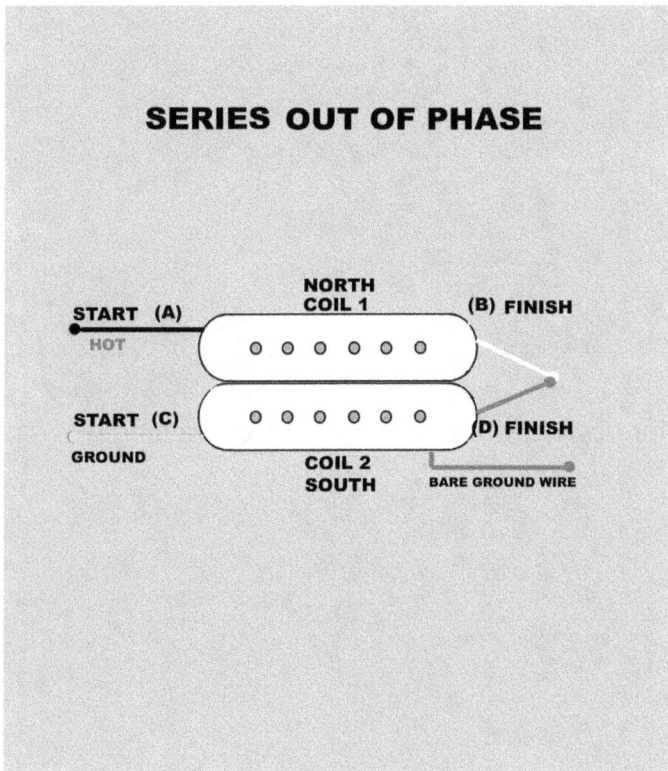

SERIES OUT OF PHASE

START (A)
HOT
NORTH
COIL 1
(B) FINISH

START (C)
GROUND
COIL 2
SOUTH
(D) FINISH
BARE GROUND WIRE

If a pickup is in series and in phase, it will sound more like a telecaster, with more highs. However, it is no longer humbucking.

SERIES IN PHASE

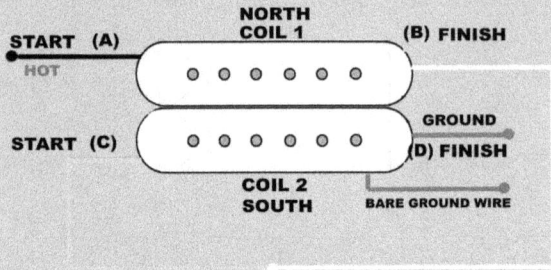

NORTH
COIL 1

START (A)
HOT

(B) FINISH

GROUND

START (C)

(D) FINISH

COIL 2
SOUTH

BARE GROUND WIRE

The parallel out of phase sound is still humbucking, but with the tone qualities of a single coil.

PARALLEL OUT OF PHASE

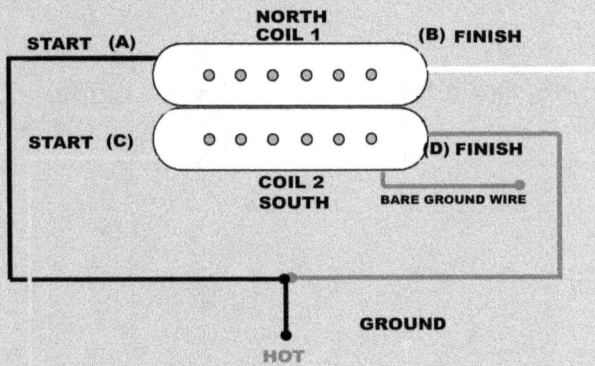

NORTH
COIL 1

START (A)

(B) FINISH

START (C)

(D) FINISH

COIL 2
SOUTH

BARE GROUND WIRE

GROUND

HOT

The parallel in phase sound is not humbucking.

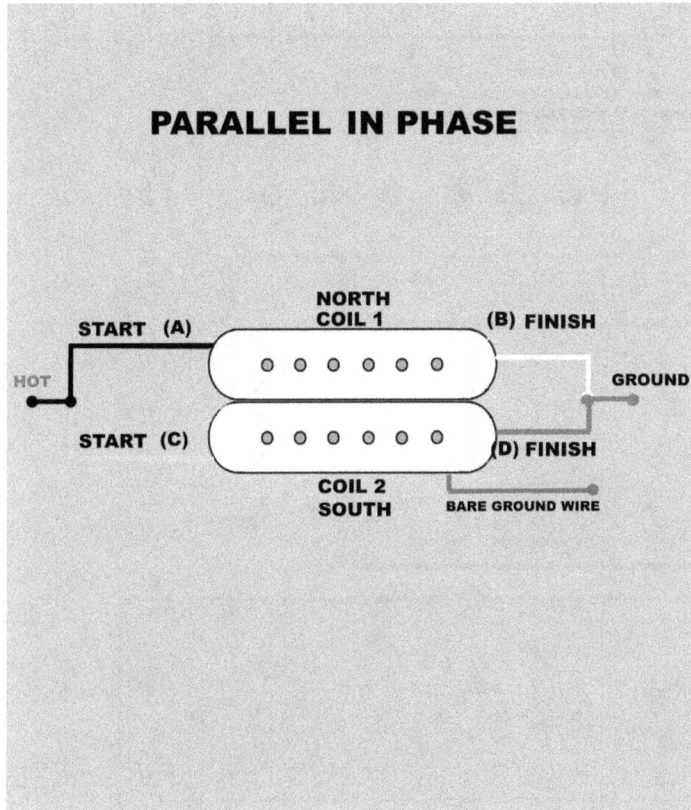

PARALLEL IN PHASE

START (A)
NORTH COIL 1
(B) FINISH

HOT

GROUND

START (C)
(D) FINISH

COIL 2
SOUTH
BARE GROUND WIRE

Question: How do you add a "bridge on" switch to a strat?
This will allow you to add 2 more tones to your strat: all three pickups on, and the neck and bridge pickups on. To add separate switching for one pickup, just add an on/on mini toggle switch, or a push pull pot to your guitar. Then send the signal to the volume pot. Check out the diagram below, or read the section on switches for more info.

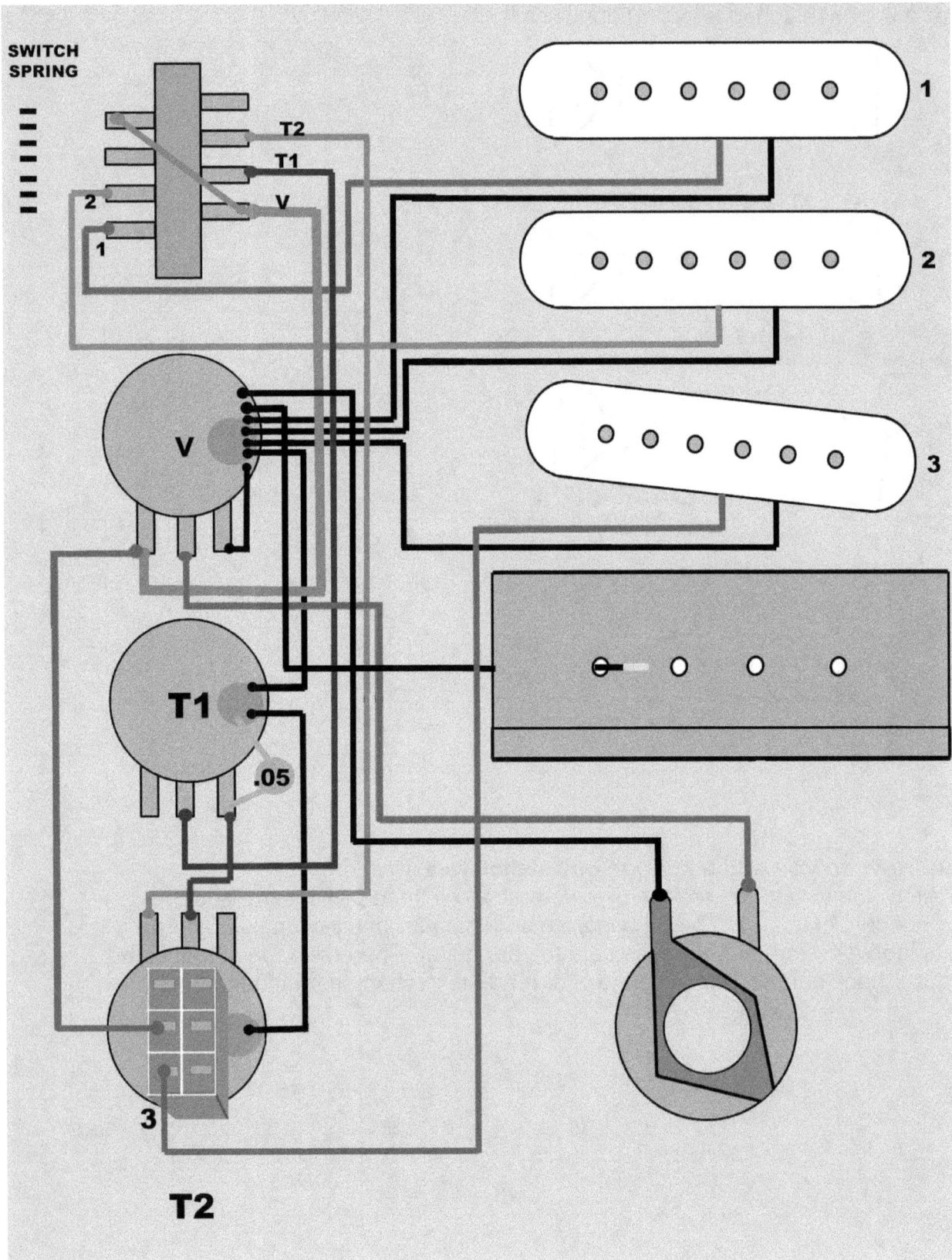

SWITCH
SPRING

T2

T1

V

2

1

V

T1

.05

T2

3

1

2

3

COLOR PDF VERSION

Download the color PDF version here: http://www.snotboards.com/stratocaster.html

Download Adobe Reader here:
http://www.adobe.com/products/acrobat/readstep2.html

Please send your questions and comments to: indyebooks@aol.com

www.ingramcontent.com/pod-product-compliance
Lightning Source LLC
La Vergne TN
LVHW081318060426
835509LV00015B/1570